A JOURNEY THROUGH TIME

A JOURNEY THROUGH TIME

The history of the British monarchy

Kings & Queens of England & Scotland:
Born, Married & Died

One

GEOFF KEEN

authorHOUSE®

AuthorHouse™ UK
1663 Liberty Drive
Bloomington, IN 47403 USA
www.authorhouse.co.uk
Phone: 0800.197.4150

Published by AuthorHouse 08/17/2015

ISBN: 978-1-5049-8980-0 (sc)
ISBN: 978-1-5049-8979-4 (hc)
ISBN: 978-1-5049-8981-7 (e)

I first got interested in kings and queens about 10 years ago when I found myself reading an historical novel about Henry VIII. It was enthralling, but it left me wanting to know more about his ancestors. I then went on to read more, it was at this point I decided to produce a concise summary of my findings into a booklet. This booklet would be a genealogical record of all the Kings and Queens of England and Scotland, starting with the first King ever recorded, King Egbert of Wessex 780 A.D, and to follow them through to Queen Elizabeth II, 1952.

For more than 2,000 years there have been Kings in England and yet this realm has been a monarchy for just over half that time. In the dark ages Kingship was nothing but tribal chieftains of Celtic or Romano British stock. In the middle of the 5th century England felt the impact of the Barbarian invasion that changed the face of Europe. Angles, Saxons and Jutes came to this country and colonised. It was here that the seven Kingdoms then evolved from, known as the Heptarchy.

In 455 A.D., Hengist founded the earliest kingdom in Kent, the other Kingdoms included Essex, Mercia and Wessex. The job of the King was to protect his people and was to pass laws for his people to abide by; the King was also expected to father sons for posterity, to ensure the stability and the succession of his Kingdom.

The main religion across the seven kingdoms was paganism, it wasn't until the late 6th century that Christianity came to Kent, it then soon spread to the rest of the Heptarchy, but there were still pagan influences up until the late middle Ages. In the 7th century Northumbria was the first Kingdom to achieve supremacy and it became the centre for the arts and religion, but all that was extinguished in the 8th to the 11th centuries due to Viking raids from Scandinavia. At the time Mercia was in the ascendant and at its peak of supremacy King Offa, who established a firm government and overseas alliances, governed Mercia. However after his death the kingdom declined due to poor leadership leaving Wessex in the ascendant. In 519 A.D a chieftain called Cerdic, who came to this country from Germany in 494/495, founded the Kingdom of Wessex and his people were proud to bear his name so they called themselves "Cerdingas". H. M. Queen Elizabeth II is a direct descendant of the Cerdics.

This book is about the monarchy and it begins with the first King recorded, King Egbert of Wessex, he was a very outstanding ruler, and was very much looked upon by lesser Kings at that time.

Not much is known about the early King's due few or no records at all, this makes information in earlier times patchy and hard to gather information form. However but as time progressed, more and more recordings are found a sound chronological order and genealogy can be produced.

King Egbert

Born between 769/780 he became "Subregulus" of Kent between 790/796. He succeeded Beorhtric as King of Wessex in 802 and was probably crowned the same year; although there are no records of his coronation. From the year 825 onwards he had established his supremacy over all the other rulers in England, and was effectively known as the overlord of all the south- eastern Kingdoms. In 829 he succeeded Wiglaf as King of Mercia, but was for some unknown reason expelled the following year. Little else is known about Egbert's brief reign.

King Egbert married, but there are no records of the date or the place. King Egbert is thought to have died on 4th February 839, and buried in Winchester Cathedral. He was succeeded by his son Ethelwulf.

King Ethelwulf

Born between 795\810 he became "Subregulus" of Kent, Essex and Surrey between 825\828. He succeeded his father as King of Wessex in July 839 and crowned at Kingston upon-Thames, Surrey. Between 855/856 he resigned Wessex to his son Ethelbald and confined his own authority to Kent, Sussex and Essex as "Subregulus".

Ethelwulf first married in 830 to Osburga. Osburga was either the daughter of Oslac of Hampshire or of the Isle of Wight, there are no records of her date of birth. She died ether in 846 or 852/855. She has sometimes been confused by historians with St Osburga, the foundress of Coventry Abbey, who died in 1018.

Ethelwulf married secondly in October 856 at Verberie sur Oise, France to Judith. Judith was the daughter of Charles I, King of the Franks by Ermentrude, daughter of Odo Count of Orleans. She was born between 843/844 and was crowned Queen of Wessex on her wedding day. In 860 she married her stepson King Ethelbald, once Ethelwulf had passes, at Chester.

However the marriage was annulled on the grounds of consanguinity. There was no children from this marriage. The date of her death is unknown. King Ethelwulf is said to have died on 13th January 858 and he was buried in Winchester Cathedral. His son Ethelbald, from his first marriage, succeeded him.

King Ethelbald

Ethelbald was the eldest son of Ethelwulf, he was born in 834, he succeeded his father as King of Wessex on 13th January 858 and was crowned shortly afterwards at Kingston-upon Thames, Surrey.

Ethelbald married in 860 to his father's widow (his stepmother), however the marriage was much frowned upon by the Church and it was annulled that same year. Ethelbald died on 20th December 860 and he was buried in Sherborne Abbey Dorset. Since he left no heirs his brother Ethelbert succeeded him.

King Ethelbert

He was Ethelbald's brother and he was born in 836. He was made "Subregulus" of Kent between 853/855. He succeeded his brother Ethelbald as King of Wessex on 20th December 860 and was crowned soon afterwards at Kingston-upon-Thames,Surrey. King Ethelbert died, unmarried and childless, either in 865 or 866. He was then buried in Sherborne Abbey, Dorset and his brother Ethelred succeeded him.

Ethelred I

Brother to both Ethelbert and Etherbald, he was born in 840. He succeeded his brother Ethelbert as King of Wessex between 865/866 and was crowned at Kingston-upon-Thames, Surrey just like his brothers.

King Ethelred married in 868 to Wulfrida. Wulfrida is a bit of a mystery as there are no know records of her origins.

King Ethelred was killed on 23rd April 871 at the Battle of Merton and was buried at Wimborne Minster, Dorset. Ethelred was a very outstanding King and after his death he was forever remembered as a saint. Since Ethelbert and Wulfrida had no know children, his brother Alfred succeeded him.

King Alfred

Known as "Alfred the Great", he was the fifth son of Ethelwulf king of the West Saxons. He was born in 849 at Wantage, Dorset Berkshire. He succeeded his brother Ethelred as King of Wessex and Danish Mercia on 23rd April 871.

Since the 790s the Vikings used fast mobile armies in shallow-draught long ships to plunder England's coasts and inland waters. These raids eventually evolved into permanent Danish settlements. In 867 the Vikings seized York and established their own kingdom in the southern part of Northumbria and in 870 the Danes attacked the only remaining independent Anglo-Saxon kingdom, Wessex. Further defeats followed Wessex and Alfred's brother was killed.

In 878 the Danes, led by King Guthrum, seized Chippenham in Wiltshire and used it as a base from which to devastate Wessex. In May 878 Alfred's army defeated the Danes at the battle of Edington. This victory proved to be the turning point in Wessex's battle for survival. Knowing he could not drive the Danes out of England Alfred concluded peace with them in the treaty of Wedmore and converted King Guthrum (King of the Vikings) to Christianity where he and his people settled as farmers. In 886 a frontier was marked out along the Roman Watling Street after a partition treaty with the Danes was negotiated; the northern and eastern areas of England came under the jurisdiction of the Danes, an area known as 'Dane-law'. Alfred now gained control of areas of West Mercia and Kent, which at one time had been beyond the boundaries of Wessex.

Alfred came to be known as 'Alfred the Great' for his valiant defence of his kingdom against a stronger enemy; also for the reconstruction of Wessex and beyond, and for securing a long lasting peace with the Vikings.

King Alfred married either in 868/869 at Winchester to Ethelswitha. After the death of King Alfred, Ethelswitha turned to religion and became a nun at St Mary's Abbey, Winchester in 901. She died in Winchester on 5th/3th December 905 and was buried in St Mary's Abbey, her remains were later removed to Winchester Cathedral. After her death she was given status as a saint.

King Alfred died in October 899 aged 50 and he was buried in Newminster Abbey, Winchester. Newminster abbey is said to be the burial place of the West Saxon royal family. His remains where later removed to Hyde Abbey, Winchester which was destroyed during the Reformation. His son Edward succeeded him.

King Edward

Known as "Edward the Elder" was born between 871/872 and he succeeded his father as King of Wessex in October 899, crowned later in 900 at Kingston-upon-Thames, Surrey. In 910 Edward defeated the Danes in Northumbria at Tettenhall; he was a bold soldier well-trained by his father Alfred and was even acknowledged by the Viking kingdom of York. In 921 the kings of Strathclyde and the Scots submitted to Edward, this was due to his military success and patient planning. Edward was the first to establish an administration for the kingdom of England.

King Edward first married Egwina. Egwina died between 901/902. King Edward then married Elfelda in 902. Elfleda was the daughter of Ealdorman Ethelhelm by his wife Elswitha. She died in 920 and was buried in Winchester Cathedral.

King Edward married for the third and final time to Edgier in 920. Edgier was the daughter of Siegel, Alderman of Kent and was born between 904/905. She died on 25th August 968 and was buried in Winchester Cathedral King Edward died on 17th July 924/925 at

Farndon-on-Dee, and he was buried in the New Minster, which he had only just built, at Winchester. It is said that his eldest son, Athelstan, may have been the son of a mistress thereby suggesting he was illegitimate, but despite this he still succeeded his father.

King Athelstan

Athelstan was born in 895; he succeeded his father on 17th July 924/925 as the first King of a united England. He was crowned on 4th September 924/925 at Kingston-upon-Themes Surrey. The monarchy in England is said to have been properly established under King Athelstan.

Athelstan was a distinguished and audacious soldier. He took York from the Danes and forced King Constantine out of Scotland and he forced the northern kings in to submission; he also eliminated all opposition in Cornwall. In 937 at the battle of Brunanburh, Athelstan led his forces in alliance with the Welsh and Danes from Dublin and defeated an invasion by King Constantine II of Scotland; in which Constantine's only son was killed. To improve alliances overseas he married off four of his half-sisters to various rulers in Western Europe.

King Athelstan died on 27th October 939 at Gloucester and he was buried in Malmesbury Abbey, Wiltshire. His half-brother Edmund succeeded him.

Edmund 1

Known as "Edmund the Magnificent", he was born between 920/922. He succeeded his half brother King Athelstan as King of England on 27th October 939 and was crowned on 29th November 939 at Kingston-upon- Themes Surrey. From 944 onwards he was the effective ruler of the whole of England and he ruled until the day he died.

Edmund first married in 940 to Elgiva. Elgiva died between, 944/946 at Shaftsbury Abbey, Dorset. Elgiva was at times described as the Abbess of Wilton and after her death she was and still is remembered as a saint. Edmund married secondly in 946 to a Ethelfleda. Ethelfleda was the daughter of Alfgar, Ealdorman of the Wilsaetas (Wiltshire) and was born at Damerham, Wiltshire. After the death of Edmund she became a nun at Shaftsbury Abbey, Dorset. She died in 975 and she was buried in Shaftsbury Abbey, Dorset.

Edmund was murdered on 26th May 946 at Pucklechurch, Dorset, when an outlaw named Liofa stabbed him whilst he was dining in his own dining hall. After only seven years on the throne he was buried in Glastonbury Abbey Somerset. His brother Edred succeeded him.

King Edred

Edred was born between 923/925 and he succeeded his brother Edmund as King of England on 26th May 946, he was then crowned on 16th August 946 at Kingston-upon-Themes, Surrey. Edred expelled the Danes from England in 954 and therefore established his authority throughout England. There are no records of him ever being married, but he did bring up Edmund's sons, Edwy and Edgar as his heirs and they both became king in turn.

King Edred died on 23rd November 955 at Frome, Somerset, and was buried in Winchester Cathedral. His bones are now in one of the mortuary chests there. His nephew Edwy succeeded him.

King Edwy

Known as "Edwy the Fair", was born between 941/943. He succeeded his uncle Edred as King of England on 23rd November 955 aged 13. Oda, Archbishop of Canterbury, crowned him King on the 26th January 956 at Kingston-upon-Themes, Surrey. King Edwy was a weak King and his authority was confined to Wessex from 958; his younger brother Edgar taking over the government of Northumbria and Mercia.

King Edwy married between 955/956 to Elgiva. The marriage was very disapproved of by the Church and it was annulled in 958. Elgiva was banished from court and she died in 959 in Gloucester. King Edwy died on 1st October 959 at Gloucester aged 19 and he was buried in Winchester Cathedral. His brother Edgar succeeded him.

King Edgar

Known as "Edgar the peaceable", he was born between 942\944. He succeeded his Brother as head of the government of Northumbria and Mercia in 958 and was thought of as King of those realms from that date. He then succeeded King Edwy as King of England on 1st October 959 and was crowned on the 11th May 973 at St Dunstan.

The coronation, which took place in Bath Abbey, followed the new form of rule by Dunstan and he based it on the European ways. This is the form of Coronation Rites used, with some changes, in the 20th century. Edgar was a firm and capable ruler whose power over other rulers in Britain was acknowledged by Welsh and Scottish kings. Edgar's late coronation was the first to be recorded in any detail and his queen was the first consort to be crowned queen of England.

King Edgar first married between 961/962 to Ethelfleda. Ethelfled, known as "Ethelfleda the Fair", was the daughter of Alderman Ordmaer by his wife Ealda. She died between 962/964 and she was buried in Wilton Abbey, Wiltshire. King Edgar then married Elfrida between 964/965. Elfrida, more often known as Alstrita or Elstrudis, was the daughter of Ordgar, Alderman of Devon, and she was born in 945 at Lydford Castle Devon. She was crowned with her husband Edgar on 11th May 973 at Bath Abbey. This was the first instance of the coronation of a Queen of England. She became a nun in 986 at Wherwell Abbey, Hampshire where she then died on 17th November 1002.

King Edgar died on 8th July 975 at Winchester and he was buried in Glastonbury Abbey, Somerset. His son Edward succeeded him.

King Edward II

Known as "Edward the Martyr", he was born in 945. He succeeded his father as King of England on 8th July 975 and was crowned at Kingston- upon-Thames that same year. King Edward never married, therefore never had any children.

King Edward II was murdered on 18th March 978 at the age of 33, by his seven-year-old half brother's "supporters"; could have possibly on the orders of his stepmother, Elfrida of Devon. He was buried in

Wareham Abbey, Dorset; his remains were later moved to Shaftsbury Abbey, Dorset. His half brother Ethelred succeeded him.

Ethelred II

Known as "Ethelred the Unraed" or "Ethelred the Redeless", (meaning 'no counsel', or that he was unwise), was the younger son of King Edgarand he was born between 966/969. He succeeded his half-brother Edward, as King of England on 18th March 978 aged 7 and he was at Kingston-upon-Themes, Surrey. In 1002 he ordered the slaughter of all Danes in England to eliminate potential treachery.

Ethelred II abdicated when the powerful Viking Sweyn of Denmark dispossessed him in September 1013 and he fled to Normandy, but he was restored to the throne, after King Sweyn's death, on 3rd February 1014. Ethelred defended the country against unscrupulous Viking raids from the 980s onwards by diplomatic alliance with the Duke of Normandy and by buying off renewed attacks by the Danes with money levied through a tax called the Danegeld. By 1012, 48,000 pounds of silver was being paid in Danegeld to the Danes camped in London.

Ethelred II first married between 980/985 to Elgiva. Elgiva, alternatively known as Elfleda, she was the daughter of Alderman Ethelbert, or of Thored, Alderman of York by his wife Hilda. She was born in 963 and she died in February 1002 at Winchester.

Ethelred II married secondly on 5th April 1002 at Winchester Cathedral. Emma was the daughter of Richard I, Duke of Normandy by his wife Gunnora and she was born between 985/987. In 1017, after the death of Ethelred II she married King Canute. Ethelred II died on 23rd April 1016 in London and he was buried in old St Paul's Cathedral, London. His tomb was lost in the Great Fire of 1666. His son Edmund succeeded him.

King Sweyn

Known as "Forkbeard" he was the son of a Danish king. He was born in 960 in Denmark. He succeeded his father as King of Denmark on 1st November 986. He was thought to have been deposed in 987, but he was restored in the year 1000. He usurped the throne of England in 1013, having defeated and deposed Ethelred II. He claimed the throne by right of conquest, but had no rightful claim to it. He was never crowned.

Sweyn began conquering territory in England in 1003, devastating much of southern and midland England. The nobility acknowledged Sweyn as king in 1013. His reign was short; he died a year later in 1014. However his son Canute the Great soon returned and reclaimed control of England.

King Sweyn first married in 990 to Gunhilda. Gunhild was the daughter of Mjeczislas I, Duke of Poland by Dubrawka. Sweyn later divorced her and She died in 1015.

King Sweyn married secondly, before the year 1000 to Sigrid, also known as Sigrith or Sigritha and called "the Haughty". She was the daughter of Skogul Toste of Sweden and she was born in Sweden. She died between 1012/1013. She has never been referred as Queen of England. King Sweyn died on 3rd February 1014 at Gainsborough, Links and was buried in England. His remains were later found and moved to Roeskild Cathedral, Denmark.

Edmund II

Known as "Ironside", he was born between 988/993. He succeeded his father as King of England on 23rd April 1016 was crowned the same month in Old St Paul's Cathedral, London.

Edmund II married in August 1015 at Malmesbury, Wiltshire to Edith. Edith and Edmund had two sons, Edward in 1016 and Edmond 1016 or 1017. Edmund II died on 30th November 1016 and he was buried in Glastonbury Abbey Somerset. Canute son of King Sweyn succeeded him by claiming the throne by right of conquest.

King Canute

He was the son of King Sweyn, and known as "Canute the Great". He was born in 995, in Denmark. He succeeded Edmund II as undisputed King of England on 30th November 1016, claiming the throne by right of conquest. He is thought to have been crowned on 6th January 1017 at Old St Paul's Cathedral, London. He succeeded his brother Harold as King of Denmark between 1018/1019 and became King of Norway by right of conquest in 1028.

King Canute's rivals (Ethelred's surviving sons and Edmund's son) fled abroad in 1018; the last Danegelds of 82,500 pounds was paid to him. Powerful and capable he consolidated his position by marrying Ethelred's widow Emma, his first English partner, and she was later appointed regent of Norway. For political reasons as well as faithful reasons, between 1027/1028, he went on a pilgrimage to Rome. His inheritance and great personality combined to make him overlord of a huge northern empire.

King Canute married on 2nd July 1017, the widow of Ethelred II. She died on 14th March 1052 and she was buried in Winchester Cathedral. Her remains now lay in one of the mortuary chests.

King Canute died on 12th November 1035 at Shaftsbury, Dorset and he was buried in Winchester Cathedral; his remains also lie in one of the mortuary chests. He was succeeded by his son Harthacanute.

King Harthacanut

Also known as Hardicanute; he was the son of King Canute by his second wife, Emma, the widow of Ethelred II. He was born in 1018 and was designated titular King of Denmark in 1028. He succeeded his father as King of Denmark on the 12th November 1035 and King of England on the same day. In 1037 in his absence from England, being preoccupied with affairs in Denmark, his authority was usurped by his half-brother Harold I and he became king of England as a whole. Harthacnut was restored again to the English throne on 17th of March 1040 after arriving back in England to find his brother Harold Harefoot dead and he himself king.

King Harthacanute died unmarried and childless on 8th June 1042 at Lambeth, London and he was buried in Winchester Cathedral. His half brother Edward, son of Ethelred II, succeeded him.

Harold I

Known as Harold Harefoot, was the son of King Canute by his first wife, Elgiva or Elfgifu. He was born between 1016/1017. He was thought to have been illegitimate, but that could have been mere political propaganda. In 1037, when King Harthacanute was still in Denmark, Harold I usurped the throne of England and was recognized as King, being crowned that same year at Oxford.

Harold I married Elgiva, her origins are unknown. Harold I died on 17th March 1040, at Oxford, and he was buried in the old Abbey, Church of St Peters Westminster. His body, after a dishonourable exhumation, was reburied elsewhere. Harold was succeeded by his half brother Harthacanute, whom he had once deposed, which in turn was succeeded by Edward, son of Ethelred II.

King Edward

Known as "Edward the confessor", he was born between 1003/1005, at Islip, Oxon. When he succeeded his half brother King Harthacanute on 8th July 1042, the crown of England reverted from the usurping Danish dynasty, to the line of Cerdic once more, and for the last time. Edward was crowned on 3rd April 1043, in Winchester Cathedral.

Edward 'the Confessor' became King; he was the only surviving son of Ethelred II, and half-brother of Hardicanute. Being brought up in exile in Normandy, Edward lacked little or no military ability. His Norman supporters caused tensions with one of Canutes most powerful earls, Godwin of Wessex. (Whose daughter, Edith, he married) these tensions resulted in the crisis of 1050/52, when Godwin assembled an army to defy Edward. With reinforcements from the earls of Mercia and Northumberland, he banished Godwin from the country, and sent Queen Edith away from the courts.

William, Duke of Normandy was designated heir; this caused hostile reaction and increased Norman influence which resulted in Godwin being brought back. Edward formed a closer alliance with Godwin's son Harold, who led the army as the king's deputy, and defeated a Welsh incursion in 1055.

During the last 15 years of Edward's reign, Prosperity was rising as agricultural techniques improved, Edward's reign was relatively peaceful, and the population rose to around one million. Edward was not an extravagant king; he lived off the revenues of his own lands, around £5,500 a year. Deeply religious, Edward was responsible for building Westminster Abbey, (Norman style) where he was eventually buried.

King Edward married on 23rd January 1045 to Edith. Edith she was the daughter of Godwin, Earl of Wessex, by his wife Gytha, and she was born in 1020. Edith is said to have been, anointed and crowned on her Wedding day, but details of the ceremony have not been recorded, her marriage to Edward was purely platonic, the King being unwilling for Religious reasons to consummate it, hence there were no children. She died on 18th December 1075, either at the Palace of Westminster or at Winchester Cathedral, and she was buried in Westminster Abbey.

King Edward died on 5th January 1066, at the Palace of Westminster, and was buried in the new, Westminster Abbey, built by his command and only recently consecrated. After Edward's death they were a succession crisis on who was rightful heir to the throne, with there being three or more potentials. But shortly after Edward's death, Harold son of Godwin crowned himself King of England, by blood right and by acknowledgment by God. On 7th February 1161, Edward the Confessor was canonized thus becoming the only King of England, ever to actually be made a saint.

Harold II

Known as Harold Godwineson, he was born between 1020/1022. He was created Earl of Anglia, in 1045. He succeeded his father as Earl of Wessex, on 15th April 1053. He was created Earl of Hereford in 1058, and was styled "Duke of the English" from 1064. He then succeeded Edward the confessor as King of England on 6th January 1066 and crowned himself at Westminster abbey, with the support of the Witan.

Harold II married in March 1064, at York to Edith. Edith she was the daughter of Alfgar, Earl of Mercia, by Edgiva or Elgiva Mallet, and she was born in 1042. After the death of Harold, she went in to exile on the Continent, where she died between 1070/1071. On the 6th of

October 1066, the Witenagemot (Council for the King) confirmed, Edward's brother-in-law Harold, Earl of Wessex, as King with no royal blood.

Hardrada, King of Norway, in alliance with Harold's alienated brother Tostig, Earl of Northumbria, Northampton, and Nottingham, invaded England in attempt to steal the throne, which he claimed by promise of king, in September 1066, using over 300 ships, but was defeated by Harold at the Battle of Stamford Bridge near York. So many were killed that only 25 ships were needed to transport the survivor's home. William, Duke of Normandy claimed that Harold had acknowledged him in 1064, as Edward's successor, had landed in Sussex, and on 14 October 1066, Harold hurried south, and his army of some 7,000 infantry and was defeated at the Battlefield of Hastings, Sussex.

Harold II was killed on 14th October 1066, at the Battle of Hastings, Sussex, he was not felled by an arrow between his eyes, as is sometimes stated, he was in fact, struck down by a blow from a sword wielded by a Norman Knight. In 1070, an abbey was built to fulfil a vow made by William I, and its high altar was placed on the spot where Harold fell. A stone memorial still marks the spot within the grounds of battle Hastings. Harold's body was later removed to Waltham Abbey, Essex, where he was finely laid to rest. William Duke, of Normandy was the victor of Hastings and succeeded him.

The Norman King's of England

Harold II was the last of the Saxon Kings of England, William I, his successor claimed the Throne of England because Edward the Confessor, had Promised him more than a decade before in 1066, that he Edward, would make him his successor. In 1064, Earl Edward was shipwrecked on the coast of Normandy, William captured him, and kept him in captivity until he had sworn to do all in his power to enforce William's claim to the English throne. William new that Harold, the most powerful man in England, next to the King, would be designated Edward's successor, and that is what did happen. In the autumn of 1065, when Edward was seen to be dying the Witan considered all the claimants, and decided that Harold was the only one with the strength and maturity to rule England. When Edward died, he left his crown to Harold, who seized the power in defiance of his oath to William.

William then gathered an army and sailed to England, and defeated Harold on 14th October 1066 at the battle of Hastings. It should have been called the battle of Senlac Ridge, because that is where it actually took place. Hastings is 11 miles away. At that time, there was only one living mail representative of the ancient Kings of Wessex, a child known as Edgar the Atheling, who was a grandson of Edmund II "Ironside" and a great-grandson of Ethelred "The Unready".

As soon as the Witan received news of Williams's victory at Hastings they set him up as King, but it quickly became obvious that Edgar's claim to the throne would be no match for William's determination to wear the crown of England. Edgar submitted to William within 6 weeks, and William was crowned King of England in Westminster Abby on Christmas Day 1066. The joining of England with Normandy brought about a new dynasty, and put England into the forefront of European affairs.

William I

Known as "William the Bastard", but later known as "William the Conqueror", he was the illegitimate son of Duke Robert I of Normandy, by Herleve (also known as Arlette), daughter of a tanner in Falaise. He was born between 1027/1028 at Falaise Castle Normandy. He succeeded his father, (the last of the Saxon Kings) as Duke of Normandy, on 22nd July 1035, despite his bad name as a bastard. In 1063, he became Count of Maine by right of conquest. He acceded to the throne of England on 25th December 1066, and he was crowned on the same day in Westminster Abbey. This was the first coronation to take place in the Abbey.

William I was knighted by his overlord, King Henry I of France, at the age of 15. From 1047, onwards, William successfully dealt with numerous rebellions inside Normandy; these rebellions involved his relatives, and threats from neighbouring nobles, and even his former ally King Henry I of France attempted to invade. In 1054, William, (a very experienced and ruthless military commander) at the Battle of Mortimer defeated the French forces. On 28 September 1066, with calm sees and favourable winds, he used 600 transport ships to carry around 7,000 men (including 2,500 cavalry) across the Channel. He landed unopposed at Pevensey, and within a few days, he had raised his fortifications at Hastings.

Having defeated an earlier invasion by the King of Norway at the Battle of Stamford Bridge near York, Harold took his forces marched south, and covered 250 miles in nine days to meet the new threat. On 14 October at the Battle of Senlac near Hastings, Harold's weary army faced William's cavalry (part of the forces brought across the Channel) supported by archers.

Despite their exhaustion, Harold's troops were equal in number, and they had the battlefield advantage of being based on a ridge above the Normans. The first uphill assaults by the Normans failed. The Normans counter-attacked with all mobility, whilst the Saxons defended as though rooted to the ground. Three of William's horses were killed under him. Harold was killed by the sword of a mounted knight, and two of his brothers were also killed. The defeated English forces fled.

William was crowned on Christmas Day 1066 in Westminster Abbey. Three months later, he returned to Normandy leaving two joint regents behind to administer his kingdom: his half-brother Odo, and the Bishop of Bayeux, the man who later commissioned the Bayeux Tapestry.

In 1068, Harold's sons raided the southwest coast of England, and there were uprisings in the Welsh Marches, Devon and Cornwall. In 1069, the Danes, in alliance with Prince Edgar the Atheling (King Ethelred's great- grandson) invaded the north and took York, but William drove the Danes back to their ships on the Humber, in a harsh campaign lasting into 1070.

To deprive the Danes of their supplies William systematically devastated Mercia and Northumbria, creating famine for the mostly peasant population, this lasted at least nine years until a treaty of peace was concluded in June 1070. The boundary with England Scotland was unclear Malcolm III was protruding into England. Yet, William moved swiftly, and moved land and sea forces north to invade Scotland. The Treaty of Abernethy in 1072 marked a truce, which was reinforced by Malcolm's eldest son being accepted as a hostage.

The good security he made in this country is not to be forgotten. He sent his own court members to conduct important trials, and maintained peace and order over his entire kingdom. The Anglo-Saxon Chronicle in 1087 declared 'he was a very stern and violent man; no one dared do anything contrary to his will, and before he died, he divided his 'Anglo-Norman' state between his sons. He bequeathed Normandy as promised to his eldest son Robert. His son, William Rufus, was to succeed him as King of England, and his third son Henry was left 5,000 pounds in silver.

William I married, either in 1050\1052 at the Cathedral of Notre Dame d'Eu in Normandy. Matilda was the daughter of Baldwin V, Count of Flanders, by Adela, daughter of Robert II, King of France. She was born in 1032, and was crowned Queen Consort on 11th May 1068, either at Westminster Abbey, or at, Winchester Cathedral. Matilda died, on 2nd November 1083, at Caen in Normandy, and was buried in the Abbey, of the Holy Trinity.

William I died on 9th September 1087, at the Priory of St Gervais, Rouen, Normandy, of wounds fighting at the siege of Mantes, and he was buried in his abbey foundation of St Stephen's Abbey, Caen Normandy. Desecrated by Huguenots (1562) and Revolutionaries (1793), the burial place of the first Norman king of England, was marked by a simple stone slab. William I was succeeded in England by his son William II and in Normandy by his son Robert.

William II

Known as "Rufus", Strong, outspoken and ruddy (hence his nickname 'Rufus'), he was born in 1057, in Normandy. He succeeded his father as King of England, on 9th September 1087, and he was crowned, on 26th September 1087, in Westminster Abbey. He never married; but is though to have had an illegitimate son Berstrand.

For 13 years, William ruled over England, his subjects welcomed him because nobody really wanted to return to the chaos of pre-Conqueror days. When he succeeded to the English throne, he could not gain full support of the barons, because a number of them thought, the throne should have been inherited, by his elder brother Robert. In 1088, led by "Odo" of Bayeux, a number of the Anglo-Norman barons rebelled against William. William with false promises recruited his English force and the rebels were defeated.

In 1089, to lay claim to Normandy, he used his English silver to buy support, having some success at first, however he was unable to claim Normandy. Relentless in his relations with his brother in 1091, under an agreement between the two brothers, William extended his grip on the duchy of Normandy. In 1092, William seized Cumbria from Malcolm Canmore, King of Scotland.

William's relations with the Church were not easy. In 1089 the Archbishop of Canterbury, Lanfranc, died, that left William to take over the Archbishops revenues. In 1093, when he was taken ill and believed to be dying himself, he decided that he should fill the post, so he appointed Anselem of Bec, as the next Archbishop; this proved to be a disaster when he found out he was not dying after all. Bec had already called for churchmen to be more politically aware, thus began a period were churchmen played a more prominent role in government.

William's unpopularity increased in 1094, when he increased taxation, sold positions of the church to the highest bidders, this left many church positions vacant, and the revenues they earned he took for himself. William made plans to recover Maine and the Vexin, both of which had been part of Normandy, but his brother lost them. It was two years later in 1099, before he succeeded in recovering them both.

In 1097, Anselem of Bec, (the Archbishop of Canterbury), decided he could not cope with another conflict with William, so he sailed to France leaving the estates of Canterbury in his hands, this was a victory for William, but that only served as a legacy of William as being a bad King.

William II he was mysteriously killed, or could have been murdered, on the orders of his brother Henry, or by Henry himself, by an arrow in his back, while he was out hunting in the New Forest Hampshire, on 2nd August 1100, he was buried in Winchester Cathedral. His brother Henry succeeded him.

Henry I

Known as "Beauclerk" or "the Lion of Justice" he was born in September 1068, at Selby in Yorkshire. He became Lord of Domfront in 1092, and Count of Coutances and Bayeux in 1096. He succeeded his brother William II, as King of England on 3rd August 1100, three days after his brother's death, and he was crowned on 5th/6th August 1100, in Westminster Abbey. He usurped the duchy of Normandy, on 28th September 1106, after defeating his brother Robert, its lawful Duke, at the Battle of Tinchebrai, in France. Henry he spent the last 28 years of his life as his brother's prisoner.

Henry was occasionally a very cruel ruler, but energetic and decisive. In the royal courts, Henry centralised the administration of England and Normandy, he used his advisers in England to act on his behalf, and his viceroys in Normandy. When he was across the Channel in Normandy, he increased the royal revenues, the official records of his exchequer (the Pipe Roll of 1130) show this and it was the first ever account to survive. Henry, he is said to have been the first Norman king to be fluent in English.

On 25th November 1120, the White Ship sank of Barfleur in Normandy, and both his legitimate sons William and Richard were drowned, This could have posed as a problem in the succession; However he did have a daughter Matilda, who married his first son William in June 1119, at Lisieux in Normandy. It was however, his nephew Stephen son of William the Conqueror's daughter Adela, who succeeded Henry after he died.

Henry I first married on 11th November 1100, at Westminster Abbey. Matilda was the daughter of Malcolm III King of Scotland, by St Margaret, a great granddaughter of Ethelred II. She was born in August, or September 1080. Matilda, was christened Edith at birth; but changed her name to Matilda, upon her marriage to Henry, as it was thought the Norman barons might not agree to a Queen with a Saxon name.

Her marriage to Henry represented the union of Norman and Saxon royal lines, she was crowned Queen Consort on the 11/14th November 1100, at Westminster Abbey, she died on 1st May 1118, at the Palace of Westminster, and was buried in Westminster Abbey.

Henry I married secondly on 29th January, or 2nd February 1121, at the Royal chapel in Windsor Castle. Adeliza sometimes known as Adeline or Alice, she was the daughter of Geoffrey VII, Count of Louvain, Duke of Lower Brabant and Lower Lorraine, by Ida, daughter of Albert III, Count of Namur and Countess of Namur in her own right. She was crowned Queen Consort on 30th January, or 3rd February 1121, at Westminster Abbey. There are no records of Adeliza's date of birth or her death.

Henry I died on 1st/2nd December 1135, at St Denis le Fermont in the Forest of Angers near Rouen, Normandy, of food poisoning and he was buried in Reading Abbey, Berkshire, (in his own foundation). His tomb was destroyed during the Reformation. Henry wanted his daughter to be his successor, so he made his baron swear allegiance to this. His nephew Stephen of Blois succeeded him.

King Stephen

He was born between 1096/1097 at Blois, France, he was made count of Mortain before 1115, and he became Count of Boulogne in right of his wife, between 1124/1125. On 22nd December 1135, he usurped the throne of England, upon the death of Henry I, who had left it to his daughter Matilda, to whom the barons had sworn allegiance. This had been given unwillingly, and it was broadly felt that women were unfit to rule, still Stephen met with little resistance, and he was crowned on 26th December 1135, at Westminster Abbey.

By 1141, his weak government saw many of his nobles disappointed and turned to Matilda, who invaded England in 1139. The country was plunged into civil war, although anarchy never spread over the whole country. He was deposed on 7th/10 April 1141, and imprisoned, while Matilda attempted to reconcile her claim to rule England. She failed in this, due to her high-handed, approach to government, which angered most of her supporters.

Stephen he was released in exchange for Matilda's illegitimate half-brother, Earl Robert, of Gloucester, and he was restored to the throne on 1st November 1141. He was again crowned, on 25th December 1141, at Canterbury Cathedral in Kent, and then again in 1146, at Lincoln Cathedral. After Earl Robert died, Matilda retired to Normandy with her husband, the Count of Anjou, the country he had conquered in 1148. In 1150, Matilda's eldest son, Henry, (whom had been given Normandy, by his father) invaded England in 1149 and again in 1153. When Eustace died later in 1153, it lead to a negotiated peace (the treaty of Wallingford) this helped Henry in inheriting the throne after Stephen died.

King Stephen married between 1124/1125 to Matilda. She was the daughter of Eustace III, Count of Boulogne, by Mary daughter of Malcolm III, King of Scotland, and sister to Matilda, wife of Henry I. Matilda was born between 1103/1105, and was Countess of Boulogne in her own right. After the death of her father, she was crowned Queen Consort on 22nd March 1136, at Westminster Abbey, she died on 2nd/3rd May 1152 at Hedingham Castle, Essex and was buried in Faversham Abbey, Kent, her tomb was destroyed during the Reformation.

King Stephen died on 25th October 1154, and was buried in Faversham, Abbey Kent; his tomb was also destroyed during the Reformation. His second cousin Henry son of the Empress Matilda succeeded him.

The Angevin or Plantagenetings of England

Henry I lost four of his children and both his legitimate heirs, when the White Ship sank off the cost of Barfleur in Normandy, in 1120. In 1121, he married a second time, but that marriage produced no children. After he died in 1135, his only surviving child was a daughter, the Empress Matilda, who at that time was married to her second husband Geoffrey count of Anjou. They married, on 3rd April, 22nd May or 17th June 1128, at Le Mans Cathedral, Anjou.

When her father died the crown of England was seized by Stephen of Blois her cousin, in defiance of the oath of allegiance, that both he and other men in power had promised Matilda that she was rightful heir and Henry's successor. Matilda did triumph but only for a short time over Stephen, in 1141, when the crown came very close to being within her reach, but she alienated her supporters by her overbearing manner, and had to retire, yet she did continue to promote her son Henry as heir to the thrown of England.

When an invading army faced her in 1153 led by Stephen, she had to bow to public opinion and name him his successor. This brought about the Treaty of Wallingford, which passed over the claims of William and Eustace, Stephen's sons, thus leaving Henry of Anjou to succeed without hindrance, to the throne the following year.

This was the beginning of the Angevin or Plantagenet dynasty. The name "Plantagenet" originated from a sprig of broom flower, Henrys father Geoffrey used to wear in his hat. The name "Plantagenet" was not formally used by the dynasty, until the 15th century. It was Richard, Duke of York, who first used it as a surname, to emphasise his claim to the throne during the Wars of the Roses. The Plantagenet's were one of the most brilliant and dynamic families of rulers the world has ever known, they ruled England for over 300 years, and for more than 200 of those years, the crown passed normally and peacefully from father to son.

Henry II

Known as "FitzEmpress" or "Curtmantle" he was born on 5th March 1133, at Le Mans, Anjou. He became Count of Touraine and Maine in 1151, and succeeded his father as Duke of Normandy and Count of Anjou on 7th September, 1151. He became Duke of Aquitaine in right of his wife on 18th May 1152. He succeeded his distant cousin Stephen, as King of England, on 19th December 1154, and was crowned the same day in Westminster Abbey.

Henry II the first Angevin King, the most powerful monarch in Europe, with lands stretching from the Scottish borders to the Pyrenees. Pope Adrian IV (the only English Pope) added Ireland to his inheritance; a new administrative and efficient system of government was now in place, and a new justice system developed.

Henry II married on 18th May 1152, at Bordeaux Cathedral, Gascony to Eleanor of Aquitaine. Eleanor she was the daughter of William X, Duke of Aquitaine, by Eleanor, daughter of Aimery 1 de Rochefoucauld, Viscount of Chatellerhault, and she was born between 1120/1122, either at the Ombriere Palace, Bordeaux, or at Belin Castle, Guienne. She succeeded her father as Duchess of Aquitaine and Countess of Saintonge, Angoumois, Limousin, Auvergne, Bordeaux, and Agen on 9th April, 1137. She was crowned Queen Consort on 19th December 1154, with her second husband Henry II, at Westminster Abbey. Eleanor died on 1st April 1204, at Fontevrault Abbey, France, the place of her burial.

During his reign, Henry had problems with both the King of France and his own appointed Archbishop of Canterbury Thomas Beckett, which the dispute ending with the murder of Thomas Beckett by a comment made by Henry when airate. Beckett was murder on

December 29th 1770 in Canterbury Cathedral, it was here on after that Beckett became a saint and his place of death became a pilgrimage.

Henry II died on 6th July 1189, at Chinon Castle in France, and he was buried in Fontevrault, Abbey, France. His son Richard succeeded him.

Richard I

Known as "Coeur de Lion" ("the Lionheart") he was born on 8th September 1157, at Beaumont Palace, Oxford. He was invested duchy of Aquitaine in 1172. He succeeded his father as King of England, and Duke of Normandy on 2nd September 1189, and was crowned on the same day in Westminster, Abbey. He fulfilled his desire for success, by going on the crusades in 1190, leaving the ruling of England to a group of his advisers. On his victories over Saladin at the siege of Acre, and the battles of Arsuf and Jaffa, concluded in 1192, by the treaty of Jaffa.

On his return from the Holy Land, Richard was captured in Austria, and released in to the Emperor Henry VII custody in 1193, and in 1194, his brother John paid a whopping great ransom of 150,000 marks of silver to the emperor, Henry VII for his release. On his return to England, he was crowned again, on 17th April 1194, at Winchester Cathedral. Richard he spent only 10 months of his 10 years reign in England.

King Philip of France was to obtain Richard's French possessions in his absence, ether through invasions or negotiations. Meanwhile Back in England, his brother John occupied Windsor Castle and prepared for an invasion of England with his Flemish mercenaries, but their mother, Queen Eleanor, took firm action, by reinforcing her garrisons, and exacting oaths of allegiance to the king. John fled back to the court off France. By the time of Richard's death, he had recovered all his lands and possessions, but his success was short-lived. His brother John became king in 1199, and Philip successfully invaded Normandy. In 1203, John retreated to England, and by 1205, he had lost all his French lands of Normandy and Anjou. Richard I married on 12th May 1191, at the Chapel of St George, Limassol Cyprus.

Berengaria was the daughter of Sancho VI, King of Navarre, by Beatrice or sanchia, daughter of Alfonso VII, King of Castile, and she was born between 1163/1165 in Navarre. She was crowned Queen Consort on 12th May 1191, in the Chapel of St George, Lemesnos, Limassol, Cyprus.

In 1230, she founded the Abbey of Le Mans, Anjou, and most likely took the veil there as a nun, possibly assuming the name in religion of Juliana. The date of her death was not recorded; she was buried in L'Espan Abbey, Le Mans, France. Her remains were later removed to Le Mans Cathedral in 1821, there was no children of her marriage to Richard I.

Richard I died on 6th April 1199, at Chalus in the Limousin, France, of the effects of an arrow wound received during the siege of Challis, and he was buried in Fontevrault Abbey, France. His brother John succeeded him.

King John

Known as "Lackland" or "Softsword", he was born on 24th December 1166, at Beaumont Palace, Oxford. He was designated King of Ireland in 1177, and he was created Count of Mortain in 1189. He was Earl of Gloucester in Right of his first wife from 29th, August 1189. He succeeded his brother Richard I as King of England and Duke of Normandy on 27th May 1199, being crowned on that day in Westminster Abbey.

Interested in law and government, and administrative affairs, he trusted no one. Disputes of heavy taxation with the Church, and a not very successful attempt to recover his French possessions, made him very unpopular. In 1209, John was excommunicated by the Pope, and in June 1215, they forced the King to sign a peace treaty (known as the Magna Carta) accepting their reforms. This limited royal powers, and guaranteed a number of rights.

The most influential clauses, called for the freedom of the Church. The most important clauses established the basis of habeas corpus ('you have the body'), i.e. that no one shall be imprisoned except by due process of law, and that 'to no one will we sell, to no one will we refuse or delay right or justice'. The Charter also established a council, to ensure that the Sovereign observed the Charter. The Magna Carta was a failure as a peace treaty the rebellious invited Louis of France to become their king. England was left in the grip of civil war, When King John died.

The Plantagenet's were dominated at home and abroad by three major conflicts. Edward I attempted to construct an empire dominated by England, and he conquered Wales and pronounced his eldest son the Prince of Wales. He then attacked Scotland, but Scotland was too elusive and kept its independence until late in the reign of the Stuart kings. The Hundred Years War began, in the reign of King Edward III, and feuds broke out between England and France. Richard II, his reign saw the beginning of the War of the Roses.

Distinctive English cultures and new social institutions also developed in this period. In the reign of Henry II, judicial reforms began, Parliament emerged and grew, Architectural style of the Normans changed to Gothic, and Salisbury Cathedral was built in this style. The majority of English cathedrals remodelled, and Westminster Abbey rebuilt. Oxford and Cambridge universities also began their origins in this period.

In 1381, began a disturbing new phenomena, the outbreak of Bubonic plague or the 'Black Death', causing huge social turbulence and killing half the country's population. The price rises and labour shortage resulted in social unrest, and the Peasants' Revolt.

King John first married on 29th August 1189, in Marlborough Castle, Wiltshire. Isabelle also called Hawise, Joan and Eleanor. She was the daughter of William, Earl of Gloucester, by Hawise, daughter of Robert de Beaumont, 3rd Earl of Leicester, and she was born between 1175/1176. She was never instated Queen of England and was divorced before 30th August 1199, on the grounds of consanguinity. Isabelle died on 14th October or 18th November 1217, and she was buried in Canterbury Cathedral, Kent. There were no children.

King John married again on 24th August 1200, in Bordeaux Cathedral Gascony to another called Isabelle. Isabelle was the daughter of Aymer Taillefer, Count of Angouleme, by Alice, daughter of Peter de Courtenay, son of Louis VI, King of France, born in 1187. She was crowned Queen Consort, on 8th October 1200, in Westminster Abbey. She succeeded her father as Countess of Angouleme in 1202, but was not formally recognized has such, until November 1206. Isabella she died on 31st May 1246, in Fontevrault Abbey, France, the place of her burial.

King John died in October 1216, at Newark Castle, Lincolnshire, and he was buried in Worcester Cathedral. His son Henry succeeded him.

Henry III

He was born on 1ˢᵗ October 1207, at Winchester Castle, Hampshire. He succeeded his father as King of England and Duke of Normandy and Aquitaine on 28ᵗʰ October 1216, he was crown on the same day in Gloucester Cathedral, with his mother's circlet, with the Crown Jewels having been lost in the River Wash. He was again crowned on 17ᵗʰ May 1220, at Westminster Abbey. In December 1259, he formally renounced the duchy of Normandy within the terms of the Treaty of Paris.

Henry was only nine when he was crowned king of England. In 1227, he took over power from his regent, and on his acceptance of the Magna Carta, order was restored. In 1230, his campaign in France failed, and he failed again in a second campaign in 1242. On 7ᵗʰ January 1254, his son Edmund (known as "Crouchback"), was nominated King of Sicily, by the Pope, to help him against the Holy Roman Emperor. However, this led to further disputes with the barons and helped unite opposition in the Church and the State. Edmund then was deprived of the Kingdom of Sicily in 1263.

Henry was a very extravagant person, and his taxation demands were much resented by his subjects. He was also a charitable person, his donations and payments for building work, included the rebuilding of Westminster Abbey, which began in 1245. In 1262, Henry renounced the Provisions of Oxford 1258, and the Provisions of Westminster 1259, and war broke out. The barons lead by Simon de Montfort, were initially successful and even captured Henry himself.

In 1264, after winning the battle of Lewes, in which Edward gave himself as a hostage, (to ensure his father abided by the terms of the peace). In 1265 de Montfort summoned the Great Parliament, this was the first time cities and burghs sent representatives to parliament. On 4ᵗʰ August 1265, he finally defeated and killed de Montfort at the Battle of Evesham, after escaping and joining forces with the lords of the Marches, and by 1267, Royal authority had been restored, and as promised he upheld Magna Carta and some of the Provisions of Westminster.

Henry III married on 14th of January 1236, at Canterbury Cathedral, Kent, to Eleanor. Eleanor was the daughter of Raymond Berenger V, Count of Provence, by Beatrice, daughter of Thomas I, Count of Savoy. Her sister Sanchia later married Henry's brother Richard. Eleanor was born between 1217/1226, at Aix-en-Provence, France, and she was crowned Queen consort on 19th/20th January 1236, at Westminster Abbey. She became a nun on 7th July 1284, in Amesbury Abbey, Wiltshire. She died on 24th/25th June 1291, in Amesbury Abbey, the place of her burial.

Henry III died on 16th November 1272, in the Palace of Westminster, and he was buried in Westminster Abbey. His son Edward succeeded him.

Edward I

Known as, "Longshanks" and "Edward the Lawgiver". He was born on 17th/18th June 1239, at the Palace of Westminster, and named by his father after his father's favourite saint, Edward the Confessor, (the last Anglo Saxon king) He was named Duke of Gascony in 1254 and Earl of Chester on 14th February 1254. He gave up the Earldom of Chester on 24th December 1264, but was restored on 4th August 1265. He succeeded his father as King of England, on 20th November 1272, and he was crowned on 19th August 1274, at Westminster Abbey.

Edward received an exhalant education, reading and writing in Latin and French, with training in both sciences and music. His mother, Eleanor of Provence, also encouraged him to spend money on the arts. At the age of 15 he sailed to Spain, for an arranged marriage to 9-year-old Eleanor of Castile, and as a wedding present Henry III (his father), gave him the duchy of Gascony, one of the few remaining French possessions of the English Angevin kings. Gascony was part of a package, Ireland, the Channel Islands and the King's lands in Wales, were also part of a package. This was to provide an income for Edward and his bride.

When Edward marched north to Elgin, and then south to Scone, his intention was to capture the Stone of Destiny, on which all the Scottish kings where crowned, he then had it sent to Westminster Abbey, where it remained for the next 700 years, before England returned it to Scotland in 1996.

In the civil war in which he fought to defend his father, he learnt some very harsh lessons from his father's failures as a king, when the Pope offered the Sicilian crown to Henry's son, it turned out to be a very expensive intervention, he went Bankrupt, and was forced to agree to the Provisions of Oxford in 1258. In exchange for some considerable reforms, the King's Council of 24 was nominated for Henry; nominated partly by the barons.

In 1261, he rejected the Provisions and turned to the king of France Louis IX. This was the only time he sided with his politically ruthless godfather Simon de Montfort. However, by the time Louis sided with Henry in 1263, civil war broke out in England, and by the end of the civil war, Edward worked hard to re-establish friendly relations between his father and the rebels and by 1267, his mission had been accomplished.

To finance Edward's Crusade to the Holy Lands, Parliament agreed in April 1270, to levy of one-twentieth of his subjects possessions. In August 1270, he left England and joined King Louis IX of France on his Crusade. They were the last crusaders to try and recover the Holy Lands. King Louis died of the plague in Tunis before Edward arrived in France, even so Edward decided to continue pilgrimage and he arrived in Acre in May 1271, with 1,000 knights. His crusade was to prove to be an anticlimax, leading to Edward's compromise truce with the Baibars, when the forces of Christian Crusaders divided.

Edward survived a murder attempt in June 1272, by the Shi'ite Muslims, and left for Sicily, never to return on crusade. Meanwhile, Henry III died, Edward succeeded him by hereditary right, and all the barons swore allegiance to him. With his military ability and his determination to bring peace to the country, making peace in Wales was to dominate the first part of his reign, which was under the strong leadership of Llywelyn AP Gruffyd, Prince of Gwynedd. By 1272, Llywelyn had taken advantage of the civil wars in England, and in 1267, the Peace of Montgomery, had confirmed his title as Prince of Wales.

In 1277 Edward decided to fight Llywelyn and easily defeated him, but Llywelyn joined his brother David in his rebellion in 1282 and war broke out again. Despite this Edward's military experience and skilful use of ships, he was able to drive Llywelyn back into the mountains of North Wales. In 1282, all attempts at Welsh independence ended, Llywelyn died and his brother David was executed.

Edward I first married on the 13th/31st October 1254, at the Abbey of Las Huelgas Burgos Castle. His wife Eleanor was the daughter of Ferdinand III, King of Castile, by Joan, daughter, of Simon of Dammartin, Count of Ponthieu and Aumale. She was born between 1244/1245 at Castile. She was crowned Queen Consort on 9th August 1274, in Westminster Abbey. She succeeded her mother as Countess Ponthieu and Montreuil in March 1279. She died on 28th November 1290, in the manor of Harby, Notts, of an unknown fever, and she was buried in Westminster Abbey.

Edward I then married Margaret on 8th/10th September 1299, at Canterbury Cathedral Kent. Margaret was the daughter of Philip III, King of France, by Mary, daughter of Henry III, Duke of Brabant, and she was born between 1279/1282 in Paris. Margaret was never crowned; she died on 14th February 1317/1318, in Marlborough Castle, Wiltshire, and she was buried in Greyfriars, Church, in London. Her tomb was lost during the Reformation. Edward I died (aged 68) on 7th July 1307, at Burgh-on-Sands, Northumberland, and he was buried in Westminster, Abbey. His son Edward succeeded him.

Edward II

He was born on 25th April 1284, at Caernarvon, Castle Wales. He succeeded his mother as count of Ponthieu and Montreuil on 28th November 1290, and he was made Prince of Wales and Earl of Chester on 7th February 1301. Edward was the first English Prince of Wales; and since then the title as always been granted to the Eldest son of the sovereign. He also became Duke of Aquitaine in May 1306. He succeeded his father as King of England on 8th July 1307, and he was crowned on 24th/25th February 1308, in Westminster Abbey.

Edward shared none of the qualities that made him as successful as his father. The barons rebelled when he tried to excluded them from power throughout his reign, many different groups of barons tried in vain to gain power and control him. Eventually he counteracted the nobles' ordinances of 1311, which was set up to limit royal control of finance and appointments. In 1314, Robert the Bruce's Scottish victory at Bannockburn made Edward very unpopular. Edward's victory in the civil war of 1321/1322, and the 1326 ordinance, which set up compulsory markets for the wool trade in 14 English, Welsh and Irish towns, did not lead to any compromise between Edward and his nobles. Edward II was deposed by an illegally convened "Parliament", on 20th January 1327.

In 1326, Edward's wife, Isabella, of France, led an invasion against her husband, and on 25th January 1327, he formally abdicated in favour of his son Edward III (this was the first time that an anointed king of England had been dethroned since Ethelred in 1013). Edward II married on 25th/28th January 1308, at Boulogne Cathedral, France.

Isabelle was the daughter of Philip IV, King of France, by Joan I, Queen of Navarre, daughter of Blanche of Artois, and she was born between 1292/1295, in Paris. She was crowned Queen consort on the 24th/25th February 1308, in Westminster-Abbey. She died on 22nd August 1358, either at Castle Rising, Norfolk, or at Hertford Castle, and she was buried in Greyfriars Church Newgate, London. Her tomb was lost during the Reformation.

Isabelle was very much involved in the planning and murder of her husband, and after his abdication, she shared the Regency with lover Roger Mortimer, Earl of March. When Edward III achieved his majority in 1330, the rulers were overthrown. Mortimer was executed, and Isabella was allowed a quiet retirement from public life.

Edward II was murdered, on 21st September 1327, at Berkeley Castle, Gloucester, after having, a red-hot spit thrust into his bowels. He was buried in Gloucester Cathedral. His son Edward succeeded him, in whose favour he had abdicated.

Edward III

He was born on 13th November 1312 at Windsor Castle and on the 24th November 1312 he was made Earl of Chester. He was also appointed Count of Ponthieu and Montreuil on the 2nd September 1325 and on 10th September 1325 he was made Duke of Aquitaine. He succeeded his father as King of England on 25th January 1327; he abdicated in favour of his son on the same day. Edward was crowned on 1st February 1327, (age 14) in Westminster Abbey.

He took over as personal ruler and assumed the role of government in his own right in 1330 after overthrowing the regents; his mother and lover Roger Mortimer. In 1337 to provide an heir to the throne with an independent income, separate to that of the sovereign or the state, he created the Duchy of Cornwall and in 1348 he founded the Order of the Garter. In 1337 at the beginning of the Hundred Years War Edward III invaded France and laid claim the to the throne of France, through his mother Isabelle daughter of Philip IV King of France, following a sea victory at Sluys, in January 1340.

In 1342, he overran Brittan and in 1346 he landed in Normandy defeating Philip IV, the King of France at the Battle of Crécy; and in 1356 his son Edward (the Black Prince) repeated his success at Poitiers. By 1360 he controlled over a quarter of France,and with his successes he won the support of his nobles and improved relations with Parliament. Although under the Treaty of Bruges 1375, Charles V of France reversed the English conquests leaving Edward with only Calais and a coastal strip near Bordeaux.

With Edward failing in France, it provoked a tremendous amount criticism at home and with the outbreaks of the Black plague 1348/1349, 1361/1362 and 1369, caused severe social disillusionment; Edward lost his daughter Joan to the Black Death on 2nd September 1348 at Loremo, Bordeaux, Gascony. In 1376 the King's advisers and the 'Good Parliament' criticised the high taxes, so severe laws were introduced in an attempt to fix wages and prices and in this time the first Speaker to represent the Commons was elected.

Edward III married, on 24th January 1328 at York Minster, Philippa. She was the daughter of William V "the Good", Count of Hainault and Holland, by Joan, daughter of Charles of France, count of Valois, and she was born between 1313/1314. She was crowned in February 1328, at Westminster Abbey; she was then again crowned on 4th March 1330. She died on 15th August, in Windsor Castle, of an illness and she was buried in Westminster Abbey.

Edward III died on 21st June 1377 at Sheen Palace, Surrey, of a stroke and he was buried in Westminster Abbey. His grandson Richard succeeded him.

Richard II

He was born on 6th January 1366/1367, at Bordeaux, Gascony, France, he was anointed Prince of Wales, Earl of Cornwall and Earl of Chester on 20th November 1376. He was also appointed a Knight of the Garter on 23rd April 1377. He succeeded his grandfather Edward III as King of England on 22nd June 1377 and was crowned at Westminster Abbey, on 16th July 1377. In 1381 the Revolt of the Peasants broke out, Richard, aged 14, bravely went and met them at Smithfield, London. Watt Tyler, the leader, was killed and the uprising was crushed within a few weeks. Well educated and highly cultured, Richard was one of the greatest royal patrons of the arts.

Built between 1097 and 1099 by William II, Richard ordered the transformation of Westminster Hall in to what it is today. The hall housed the Courts of Justice until 1882 and it was the ceremonial and administrative centre of the kingdom.

Richard upset many vested interests and his dependence on favourites provoked resentment. In 1388, headed by the King's uncle of Gloucester, a group of hostile lords sentenced many of his favourites to death, and forced Richard to renew his coronation oath. In 1394 when his Queen Anne of Bohemia died his subsequent arbitrary behaviour alienated his subjects further.

In 1397 Richard did take his revenge by arresting or banishing his opponents; Henry of Bolingbroke, his cousin, was also banished. On the death of John of Gaunt, Henry's father, he confiscated the Duchy of Lancaster, which was a state within a state, and divided them among his supporters. In 1399, with the help of the former Archbishop of Canterbury, Henry of Bolingbroke returned to claim his father's inheritance whilst his father Richard was away in Ireland. On his return Henry captured and deposed Richard, and Bolingbroke was crowned King. Henry of Bolingbroke, usurped the throne as Henry IV, when Richard formally abdicated on 29th September 1399.

qRichard II first married in January 1382 at St Stephens Chapel in the Palace of Westminster, to Anne. Anne was the daughter of Charles IV, Holy Roman Emperor, by Elizabeth, daughter of Bogislaw V, Duke of Pomerania and she was born on 11th May 1366, at Prague, Bohemia. She was crowned Queen of England on 22nd January 1382 at Westminster Abbey, and she was appointed a Lady of the garter the same year. Anne died on 7th June 1394 at Sheen Palace, Surrey, of the Plague and was buried in Westminster Abbey. There were no children.

Richard II married secondly in November 1396 at St Nicholas Church, Calais, France to Isabelle. Isabelle was the daughter of Charles VI, King of France, by Isabelle daughter of Stephen II, Duke of Bavaria-Ingolstadt and was born on 9th of November 1389 at the Palace of the Louvre in Paris. She was appointed a lady of the Garter in 1396 and she was crowned in January 1397 at Westminster Abbey. She died on 13th September 1409 at the Chateau of Blois, France and she was buried in St Laumer's Abbey, Blois, France, her remains were later removed to the Church of the Celestines. There was no issue of her marriage to Richard II.

Richard II died in prison at Pontefract Castle, Yorkshire and was buried in King's, Langley church Herts, but was moved some 13 years later in 1413 to Westminster Abbey. He was succeeded by his cousin; Henry IV of Bolingbrook.

The later Plantagenet's: the Houses of Lancaster and York

Edward III had eight sons, four of them in later life had sons of their own. The eldest became the Prince of Wales known to history as the black Prince, who was the father of Richard II. Richard. Although his entitlement to the throne was never in dispute, he was a weak and not a very stable ruler. This led to his deposition by Henry of Bolingbroke in 1399, Bolingbrook's usurpation of the throne and Richard's murder the following year. Bolingbroke from that day forward was known as Henry IV; who was the son of John of Gaunt, Duke of Lancaster and the third son of Edward III. However, the rightful heir to the throne was Edmund Mortimer, Earl of March and Ulster.

There is no doubt Edmund had a better claim to the throne than Bolingbroke, but Edmund was only a child and Bolingbroke was a good soldier. England at the time needed a firm ruler, so they set aside the claim of Edmund Mortimer while the House of Lancaster usurped the throne. Edmund died in 1425 and his sister inherited his claim to the throne. It was Anne's child, Richard duke of York, who first used the surname Plantagenet.

For about 50 years, the Henrys ruled England from the house of Lancaster under Henry IV, Henry V and Henry VI. Henry V was the executioner of Richard Earl of Cambridge, who was the husband of Anne Mortimer and son of Edmund of Langley, Duke of York, and the fourth son of Edward III. Richard of Cambridge tried to overthrow the fifth Henry, but was discovered and eliminated on the eve of the campaign; this would see the English victorious at Agincourt.

Henry VI married Margaret of Anjou but the marriage produced no issue at first. Then in 1453 the Queen produced a son, who was created

Prince of Wales the following year, but many of the Duke of York's followers wondered about the child's paternity. Yet it was Henry IV's bad government rather than this that precipitated the dynastic struggle which was known as the war of the Roses. The main protagonists, whilst in the gardens of the Inns of Temple in London, who were hotly disputing the question of the succession, are said to have picked roses from a bush to use as emblems, a white rose for York and a red rose for Lancaster.

The court party headed by the king himself was deeply resented by York, but only later did he assert his superior claim to the throne. Thirty years of intermittent hostilities broke out in 1455; the first battles were not very decisive. Then in 1460, he died at the battle of Wakefield; and his son, Edward, Earl of March, took up the cause. He won a decisive victory, at Towton the following year. It was then that he was accepted as King of England, and he was crowned in Westminster Abbey.

Edward IV was a strong and decisive King, but he made the fatal mistake of marrying a commoner, Elizabeth Woodville, who brought a number of rapacious relatives, all looking for land and wealth. This angered the Earl of Warwick, "the Kingmaker", who was his best supporter. Warwick then made an alliance with, Margaret of Anjou, and that brought about the "redemption" of Henry VI, Edward fled, but he soon rose; and returned with an army to march upon his enemies for the last time.

Warwick was killed at the Battle of Barnet in April 1471, and Margaret's Lancastrian forces fought the battle of Tewkesbury in May 1471, the same month Henry VI died in mysterious circumstances in the Tower of London. At last, the House of York was securely established on the throne. Edward IV died on 9th April 1483, probably worn out by the pleasures of the bedchambers; leaving Edward V has his heir, a boy of only 12 years old. The government was now in the very capable hands of his brother, Richard, Duke of Gloucester. Gloucester announced soon after, that his brother's marriage to Elizabeth Woodville had been bigamous, and they were bastards and unfit to inherit the crown.

The Protector then found out that Edward had been seeing another woman whilst he was married to Elizabeth, so the crown was offered to Gloucester, who accepted it, and he was crowned as Richard III in July 1483. Edward V and his brother as customary, before a King was crowned, were living in the tower of London, but they disappeared, and controversy has raged ever since: the evidence points to them being murdered on the orders of Richard III.

Richard had not been crowned very long, when his son died in 1484, and the following year his wife died in 1485, that left his sister's son John de la Pole, Earl of Lincoln as his heir. Seemingly, England was never destined to have a King John II, because all the descendents were from the family of Edward III, who had either died out, or been bard from the succession, by Act of Attainder. There was a young member of the Beauforts in exile in France, who was the issue of John of gaunt, by his mistress Katherine Swynford (they later married).

The Beauforts might have been legitimate after their parent's marriage, but Letters Patent of Henry IV barred them from the succession, however this technicality did not deter Henry Tudor, an "unknown Welshman" who invaded England in 1485, with a foreign army, and defeated Richard III at the Battle of Bosworth. He then had himself crowned on the battlefield as King Henry VII with a circlet that had fallen from the head of the dead Plantagenet King of England.

He was the last Plantagenet King of England. The Tudor dynasty was born, and Henry VII united the rival Houses of Lancaster and York, by marrying Elizabeth, daughter of Edward IV. The Battle of Stoke ended the Wars of the Roses in 1487, when John, Earl of Lincoln, perished. It was another 50 years before the tragedy of the House of York ended, after nearly all of the members had been brutally eliminated, by the usurping Tudors.

Henry IV

He was born either on the 3rd April 1367 at Bolingbroke Castle, Lincoln. He was appointed a Knight of the Garter on the 23rd April 1377 and he was made Earl of Derby on 16th July 1317. He was created Earl of Northampton and was Earl of Hereford in right of his wife from 22nd of December 1384. He was created Duke of Hereford, on 29th September 1397, and Duke Lancaster and Earl of Lincoln on 3rd February 1399. He usurped the throne of England upon the abdication of Richard II on 30th September 1399 and he was crowned on 13th October 1399, at Westminster Abbey.

Exiled for life by Richard II in 1399, Henry IV spent much of his reign fighting to keep his lands. Recognition of his claim went unrecognised on his usurpation and he remained unrecognised by Charles VI of France, as King of England. In 1400, there was another outbreak of the plague, at the same time led by Owen Glendower the people of Wales revolted. In 1403 the Percy's of Northumberland, Henry's supporters, turned against him and they in turn turned to Glendower, however at the Battle of Shrewsbury the Percy's and the Welsh were defeated by Henry. In 1405 the Archbishop and some other rebels at York were executed. Although Henry had gained control of the country by 1408 he was smitten by illness and from 1405 onwards his son Henry played the role off governing the country.

Henry IV first marriage's date and venue were uncertain, but he married Mary de Bohun. Mary was the daughter of Humphrey de Bohun, Earl of Hereford, Essex and Northampton, by Joan, daughter of Richard FitzAlan, Earl of Arundel and she was born between 1369/1370. She was appointed a lady of the Garter in 1388. She died on 4th June 1394 at Peterborough Castle in childbirth and she was buried in St Mary's Church, Leicester.

Henry IV married secondly by proxy on 3rd April 1402 at Eltham Palace, Kent and in person on 7th February 1403, at Winchester Cathedral to Joan. Joan she was the daughter of Charles II, King of Nave by Joan, daughter of John II, King of France and she was born in 1370. She was crowned Queen Consort on 25th/26th February 1403 at Westminster Abbey and was appointed a lady of the Garter in 1405. She died either in 1437 at the Dover House on the royal manor of Havering-atte-Bower, Essex and she was buried in Canterbury Cathedral, Kent. Henry IV died on 20th March 1413 from a disease in the Jerusalem Chamber in Westminster Abbey and he was buried in Canterbury Cathedral. His son Henry succeeded him.

Henry V

He was born either on 16th September 1387 at Monmouth Caste. He was appointed Prince of Wales, Duke Cornwall and Earl of Chester and Prince of Aquitaine on 15th October 1399. He was appointed a Knight of the Garter in 1399 and was selected Duke of Aquitaine in

1399. He was made Duke of Lancaster on 10th November 1399. He succeeded his father as King of England on 21st March 1413 and he was crowned on 9th April 1413 in Westminster Abbey. He was designated heir to the throne of France on 21st May 1420, but he did not enjoy it for long, he died 2 years later in 1422.

Henry V laid claim to the French crown not long after his accession. Fighting alongside his father at the battle of Shrewsbury, he gained military experience whilst in his teens, and he turned out to be Stern and ruthless as well as being a brilliant general. In 1415 he sailed to France and captured Harfleur. His offer of personal combat to the Dauphin of France as his predecessors, Richard I and Edward III had made similar offers, was refused. However he defeated the French at the Battle of Agincourt in alliance with Burgundy. With the assistance of his brother, the Dukes of Clarence, Bedford and Gloucester, he gained control of Normandy and by the Treaty of Troyes 1420, he became heir to the French throne and married Katherine, Charles VI' daughter.

Henry V married in 1420 in Troyes Cathedral, France to Katherine. Katherine she was the daughter of Charles VI, King of France by Isabelle daughter of Stephen II, Duke of Ingolstadt-Bavaria and she was born on 27th October 1401 at the Hotel de St Pol, Paris. She was crowned in Westminster Abbey on 23rd/24th February 1421. She died on 3rd January 1437 at the Abbey of St Saviour, Bermondsey, London, in childbirth and she was buried in Westminster Abbey.

Henry V died of dysentery in 1422 at the Castle of Bois-de-Vincennes, France and he was buried in Westminster Abbey. His son Henry succeeded him.

Henry VI

Henry was born on 6th December 1421 at Windsor Castle and is said to have been designated Duke of Cornwall from birth. He succeeded his father as King of England on 1st September 1422 and he succeeded his grandfather, Charles VI of France as King of France on 11th October 1422, under the terms of the Treaty of Troyes1420, which settled the French succession. Henry was crowned in Westminster Abbey in November 1429 and again at the Cathedral of Notre Dame in Paris in December 1431. He claimed the rite of personal ruler on

12th November 1437 and on 4th March 1461 he was deposed in favour of Edward VI, Duke of York, but was restored to the throne on 30th October 1470; this was known as the "Redemption", he was again deposed in favour of Edward VI on 11th April 1471.

Henry's uncles Cardinal Beaufort and the Duke of Gloucester dominated his minority. The Duke of Bedford, another uncle who was Regent of France, died in 1435, at the same time Burgundy broke the alliance with England. English rule collapsed in northern France and it proved too difficult for Henry to maintain a dual monarchy from England. In 1450 with the successes of the Dauphin and Joan of Arc, England's French possessions and Normandy was lost.

Henry's interest in education founded Eton and King's College, Cambridge. Henry became ill in 1453 and in 1454, Richard, Duke of York became Protector. In 1455 Henry finally recovered, but a civil war broke out between the Yorkshire and Lancashire, known as the Wars of the Roses. Queen Margaret of Anjou and Henry were determined to fight for the Lancastrian cause. The Duke of York asserted his claim to the throne because he was a descendent of Edward III's second surviving son and Henry VI was a descendent of Edward's third surviving son.

The Duke of York was killed, in 1460, at the Battle of Wakefield and in 1461 his son Edward, a very able commander, defeated the Lancastrian at the Battle of Towton; were 28,000 men died out of nearly 120,000. The gates of London now opened to the Yorkshire forces, Henry and Queen Margaret fled to Scotland. However in 1465 Henry VI was captured and imprisoned in the Tower of London; it was some 5 years later in 1470 before he was restored to the throne. In 1471 his son Edward, Prince of Wales was killed at the Battle of Tewkesbury and when Edward IV regained the throne Henry IV was put to death in the Tower of London.

Henry VI married by proxy on 24th May 1444 at the Cathedral of St Martin, Tours, France and in person on 23rd April 1445 at Titchfield Abbey, Hampshire. Margaret was the daughter of Rene, Duke of Anjou and King of Naples and Sicily by Isabella, Duchess of Lorraine and daughter of Charles I, Duke of Lorraine. She was born on 23rd March 1429, at Pont-a-Mousson, Lorraine; she was crowned, in Westminster Abbey on 30th May 1445. She died on 25th August 1482, at Chateau Dampierre, Anjou, and was buried in St Maurice's Cathedral, Angers, Anjou.

Henry VI was murdered on 27th May 1471, in prison in the Tower of London, and was buried in Chertsey, Abbey, Surrey, but was moved to St George's Chapel, Windsor, in 1485. His distant cousin Edward IV had already succeeded him.

Edward IV

He was born on 28th April 1442, at Rouen, France, and was known has the Earl of March, up until the 30th December 1460, when his father Richard was killed at the battle of Wakefield. In November 1459, he forfeited all his honours by Act of Attainder; but was restored, in October 1460, when on 30th December 1460, he succeeded his father as Duke of York, Earl of Ulster and Cambridge. He was proclaimed King of England, by Parliament on 4th March 1461, after the deposition of Henry VI, and he was crowned on 28th June 1461, at Westminster Abbey. Edward he was deposed in favour of Henry VI, on 3rd October 1470, but was restored on 11th April 1471.

Despite the short return to the throne of Henry VI, Edward IV was able to restore order, supported by the Earl of Warwick, 'the Kingmaker', who was killed at the Battle of Barnet in 1471. With a shrewd display of force to exert pressure, he was able to make peace with France, and in 1475, Edward reached a profitable agreement with Louis XI at Picquigny. To enforce justice he relied on his own personal control in government, by sitting in person 'on the bench' in judgement. To restore his family's fortunes, he successfully traded in wool, enabling him to live of his own, and freeing him from dependent subsidies from Parliament.

When Edward IV rebuilt St George's Chapel at Windsor, he probably saw it as a mausoleum for the Yorkist's. He also built the great hall at Eltham Palace, and in the British Library is his unique collection of illuminated manuscripts, which is the only intact medieval royal collection to survive.

Edward IV married on 1st May 1464, at the Manor of Grafton Regis, Northants. Elizabeth she was the daughter of Richard Woodville 1st Earl Rivers, by Jacquetta of Luxembourg, and she was born in 1437. She was crowned Queen Consort, on 26th May 1465, at Westminster Abbey. Her marriage to Edward IV was declared invalid, on 25th June 1483, by the Act of Parliament, known as "Titulus Regius", because of

Edward's alleged promise to marry Lady Eleanor Butler, her children were at the same time declared illegitimate, and unfit to inherit the crown. By the time of the first Parliament of Henry VII, later proved the marriage as valid in October 1485, and the children were restored with all honours. Elizabeth she died, on 8th June 1492, at St Saviours Abbey, Bermondsey, London, and was buried in St George's Chapel, Windsor.

Edward IV died on 9th April 1483, at the Palace of Westminster, and was buried in St George's Chapel, Windsor. His son Edward succeeded him.

Edward V

He was born either on 1st/2nd or the 4th November 1470, in the Sanctuary, of Westminster Abbey. He was created Duke of Cornwall on 17th July 1471. and he was created Prince of Wales and Earl of Chester on 25th/26th June 1471, He was appointed a knight of the Garter, on 15th May 1475, and created Earl of March and Earl of Pembroke on 8th/18th July 1479. He succeeded his father as King of England, on 9th April 1483. Edward he was declared illegitimate by Act of parliament, on 25th June 1483, and was deposed that same day.

Edward V was only 12 when he succeeded to the thrown, so his uncle Richard, Duke of Gloucester, was made his Protector. Richard and his brother Edward IV had been loyal throughout to each other, and throughout their Brother George's rebellion (the Duke of Clarence) that in 1478 was executed, reputedly by drowning in a barrel of Malmsey wine, and suspicions were put on the Woodville's for Clarence's death. An attempt by Elizabeth Woodville to take over power was fowled when Edward V and his uncle Richard came to London in May, for his coronation that was fixed for, June 22nd 1478. However, in mid-June Richard assumed the throne as Richard III. Edward V he was declared illegitimate by Act of Parliament on 25th June 1483, and deposed the same day. He was last seen alive within the precincts of the Tower of London in July 1483.

Edward V he was murdered (supposedly) on 3rd September 1483, in the tower of London, at the same time, as his brother, Richard. Rumours at the time accused Richard III of their murders, but the evidence could only have been circumstantial. The boys thereafter were known as ("the Princes in the Tower"). In 1674, bones believed to have been those of Edward and his brother was discovered beneath a staircase during excavations in the Tower. They were removed and buried in Westminster Abbey in 1678. His uncle, Richard of Gloucester, succeeded him.

Richard III

He was born on 2nd October 1452, at Fotheringhay Castle, Northants. He was created Duke of Gloucester, on 1st November 1461, and was appointed a Knight of the Garter on or just before the 4th February 1466. He acceded to the throne of England on 26th June 1483, after the deposition of his nephew Edward V, and he was crowned on 6th July 1483, in Westminster Abbey. Richard III usurped the throne from the young Edward V, who disappeared while under their uncle Richard, Duke of Gloucester, protection.

Richard III attempted reconciliation with the Yorkist's by showing consideration to those thrown from office by Edward IV. In 1484, the first laws were passed during his reign, and they were all written entirely in English. Before becoming king, Richard had a strong alliance in the north, but this served only to increase resentment in the south. Richard eventually concluded a truce with Scotland, hoping to reduce his commitments up north, but to no avail, resentment grew. On 7th August 1485, Henry Tudor arrived in Milford Haven in Wales to claim the throne in a two-hour battle at Bosworth. On 22 August 1485, (assisted by Lord Stanley's army of around 7,000), Henry's forces defeated Richard's larger army.

Richard III married on 12th July 1472, in Westminster Abbey. Anne she was the daughter of Richard Neville, Earl of Warwick, by Anne, daughter of Richard de Beauchamp, Earl of Warwick, and she was born on 11th June 1456, at Warwick Castle. She was crowned Queen consort on 6th July, at Westminster Abbey: she died on 16th March 1485, at the Palace of Westminster, probable of tuberculosis, and was buried in Westminster Abbey.

Richard III was killed and buried without a monument, on 22nd August 1485, defending his crown and his Kingdom, at the battle of Bosworth Field in Leicester: against the forces of Henry Tudor, and he was buried in Greyfriars Abbey, Leicester. Richard's bones were scattered during the English Reformation. Richard he was the last Plantagenet King of England. His distant cousin Henry Tudor succeeded him.

The Tudors

The Tudors ruled England for 118 years, and they all seem to have come from bastard stock. Henry VII's mother Margaret Beaufort was a descendant of John of Gaunt, and his mistress Katherine Swynford. Edmund Tudor, Henry V's father was the son of the affair between Henry V's widow, Katherine and the Welsh squire, Owen Tudor, they may have married in secret, but there are no records to prove this. Henry VII's mother was only 13 year old when he was born; he being her only child. His father never saw the child; he died shortly before his birth.

Edward IV exiled Henry, when he was still a child, and he spent his youth in the courts of France and Brittany with his uncle, him being a staunch supporter of Jaspar Tudor, both of course were utterly loyal to Henry VI, and the house of Lancaster, and after the death of Henry VI and his son Edward. Henry Tudor was seen by many as the natural heir to the Lancastrian claim to the throne of England: Despite him not being intelligent enough for such a role, but there was no one else with the right bloodline.

On Christmas Day 1483, in the Cathedral of Rennes in Brittany, he vowed to marry Elizabeth of York, daughter of Edward IV, and unite the red and white roses of Lancaster and York. Henry at this time must have known that her brothers were dead. Elizabeth had been declared a bastard, and if she was to be declaring her father's legitimate heir, it cold only be so, if both her brothers died before her.

Henry Tudor defeated Richard III at the battle of Bosworth two years later, on 22 August 1485, and was made King of England. The following year, he kept his vow, and married Elizabeth in January 1486. Henry's crown was his by right of conquest and descent, not through his marriage to Elizabeth of York. Thus was founded the Tudor dynasty, and it was to be one of the most splendid and successful of all the English

Royal Houses, but there was no niceness about them, they did only what they thought necessary, all be it ruthlessly and very thoroughly, and thousands of people were executed for heresy or treason.

When Elizabeth died in 1603, the government assumed most of the power. England now emerged from a mediaeval world to a modern state, proud and prosperous. Henry VIII severed all links with the Church of Rome after he declared himself Head of the Church of England, and under Elizabeth, the Protestant Anglican Church became firmly established. Trade flourished when Voyages of discovery started to open up the wider world.

The Tudors were very capable and powerful monarchs, but there were too many members of the House of York still alive for them to feel secure on the throne, there would be threats from the Grey family and also by Mary Queen of Scots, but their worst threat to the throne came from the House of York. When Henry VII acceded to the throne there were still 18 people alive with more right to the throne than he was; that included his own wife and mother. By the year 1510, there had been 16 more born with Yorkist blood, many of them female, and there was no law in England to stop them from sitting on the throne. Unlike France, where women were thought of as unfit to rule over men, so no one really thought of a Yorkist woman sitting on the throne of England.

This was left to the Tudors, to prove that a woman could rule successfully. It was the men of the House of York, which was the biggest threat to the Tudors. Henry VII and Henry VIII, both knew of their weakness of their claim to the throne and dealt ruthlessly with any would be rivals, some died young and only eight survived to be serious contenders for the throne, two chose to retire, and were left unmolested. Two died fighting in battles, one of them an exile fighting for a foreign country, and the remaining four executed.

The House of York, was virtually eliminated when Henry VIII ordered Richard III to be put to death at the age of 67, he was beheaded in a very horrific manner, being charged for treason for no apparent reason. The other members of the family were locked up in the Tower of London and left to rot. Henry needed a son and heir and took drastic measures to get one, by taking six wives in the process beheading two of them and divorcing two more.

Henry finely had a son, Edward VI, but he did not live long enough to marry. This left no alternative, but for the country to turn to a female to be its ruler, was Mary I. That left her sister Elizabeth to be the next to rule England She had a long and glorious reign, but she never married and that left the country guessing as to whom she would name as her successor; it turned out to be her cousin, James VI of Scotland, a descendant of Henry VII, the founder of the House of Stuart 1603.

Henry VII

He was born on 28th January 1457 at Pembroke Castle in Wales, and he was Earl of Richmond from birth. Being his Father's posthumous child he was deprived of the earldom of Richmond, in August 1462. He succeeded Richard III has King of England on 22nd August 1485, after the battle of Bosworth, and was crowned on 30th October 1485, in Westminster Abbey.

Richard III's usurpation alienated Henry, although he had the support of the Lancastrians and Yorkists. By marrying Elizabeth of York in 1486, Henry secured his position, but he was still troubled by revolts. Sometimes pretenders such as Perkin Warbeck, and Lambert Simnel, were involved. In 1485, he formed a personal bodyguard, they were known as the 'Yeomen of the Guard', who are still in existence today.

To tighten royal administration and increase revenues, he used traditional methods of government, this also increased the power of the monarchy, and Royal income rose to £142,000 from £52,000. By the end of Henry's reign, little or no co-operation was needed from Parliament. Records show that Parliament sat for some ten and a half months during Henry's reign.

To help maintain peace, Henry used royal marriages to establish his dynasty. Out of his eight siblings, he married his daughter, Margaret to James IV of Scotland. After James died, she married Archibald Douglas, 6th Earl of Angus in 1514. He married his other daughter Mary, to Louis XII of France. She married secondly Charles Brandon, Duke of Suffolk in 1515.

Henry VII married on 18th January 1486, in Westminster Abbey. Elizabeth she was the daughter of Edward IV by Elizabeth Woodville, and she was born on 11th February 1466, at the Palace of Westminster. She was crowned Queen consort, on 25th November 1487, in Westminster

Abbey. She died, on 11th February 1503, in the Tower of London in childbed, and she was buried in Westminster Abbey. Henry VII died on 21st April 1509, at Richmond Palace, Surrey, and he was buried in Westminster Abbey. His son Henry succeeded him.

Henry VIII

He was born on 28th June 1491, at Greenwich Palace Kent. He was created Duke of York on 31st October 1494, and was appointed a Knight of the garter on 17th May 1495. He became heir to the throne, on the death of his elder brother, Prince Arthur, and as Duke of Cornwall on 2nd April 1502, He was created and invested Prince of Wales and Earl of Chester on 18th February 1504, at the Palace of Westminster. He succeeded his father as King of England on 22nd April 1509, and was crowned on 24th June 1509, in Westminster Abbey. In 1521, he added to the royal title "Fade Defender" (Defender of the Faith"), and it was past by Pope Leo X.

This title is still born by the Queen today. He also in 1542 claimed the title King of Ireland. In his youth, Henry was highly intelligent, and was very good at athletics. He spoke French, Latin and Spanish, and was very religious: he heard three masses daily. He was also fond of tennis, and extremely fond of hunting. He wrote both books and music, and he was a lavish patron of the arts. His best-selling book went through 20 editions in England and Europe. In 1515, Thomas Wolsey, an Ipswich butcher's son, became Lord Chancellor, (one of the most powerful ministers in British history) because Henry had little interests in government business or administration. In addition, in 1515, Wolsey was appointed Cardinal, and given papal Brief approval, this allowed him to by-pass the Archbishop of Canterbury, and 'govern the Church in England.

Western Europe, where Henry's foreign policy were focused, was a shifting pattern of alliances, centred round the Holy Roman Emperor, and the kings of Spain and France. Related to all three through his wife Catherine, who was Ferdinand of Aragon's daughter, in 1514, his sister Mary married Louis XII of France, and the Holy Roman Emperor, Charles V was Catherine's nephew.

Peace was finally made with France in 1520, Henry VIII he increased the size of the navy from 5 to 53 ships, with his investments. The Mary Rose was one of his ships; it now lies in the Portsmouth Naval Museum. Dominated by two issues, the second half of his reign was the succession and the Protestant Reformation, which led to the formation of the Church of England. In 1499, because it had never been legal, Henry tried to persuade the Pope to grant him an annulment of his marriage to Anne Boleyn, (the sister of one of his many mistresses) but Wolsey failed to gain the Pope's agreement. He died before he could be dismissed arrested, and brought to trial.

To obtain the divorce through pressure failed, Thomas Cromwell, Wolsey's successor, and Henry's chief adviser, (from 1532 onwards) turned to Parliament to decide the issue. The result was to bringing about the English Reformation, by cutting back papal power, through a series of Acts by Parliament. An Act against Annates in 1532, was a clear warning to the Pope, revenues were under threat. Cranmer was made Archbishop of Canterbury in 1532. In May 1533, Cranmer declared Henry's marriage invalid, and Anne Boleyn was crowned queen.

Henry decided to break with the Roman Catholic Church, following the Popes response of excommunication, and Parliamentary legislation. Fobbing appeals to Rome, with an Act in restraint of appeals, stating that England was an empire, governed by one supreme leader the king, who possessed entire' authority within the realm, and that no judgements or excommunications from Rome were valid.

An Act of Submission of the Clergy and an Act of Succession followed, together with an Act of Supremacy in 1534, which recognised that the king was 'the only supreme head of the Church of England, called Anglican Ecclesia'. Clergy, office-holders and others had to choose their allegiance, following the breach between the king and the Pope, the most famous being Sir Thomas More, who was executed for treason in 1535. To pay for his new foundations, to build colleges at Oxford and Ipswich, Wolsey closed down some of the small monastic communities, Crown revenues doubled for a few years, when in 1535/36, another 200 smaller monasteries were dissolved, by statute, followed by the remaining greater houses in 1538/1540.

Henry's second marriage to Ann in 1533, raised hopes for a male heir, but Anne Boleyn failed to produce a male child, Anne was charges for treason. Henry's third wife Jane bore him a son, Edward VI, who was educated the Protestantism way rather than Catholicism way. Thomas Cromwell proved an effective minister, in bringing about the royal divorce and the English Reformation. Despite being made Earl of Essex in 1540, he was arrested and executed three months later.

In the last seven years of Henry's reign, know one emerged to succeed the Earl. Henry turned his attention to France once more, despite assembling an army of 40,000 men, his French campaign failed, when only the town of Boulogne was captured. The war contributed to only one thing; increased inflation. Henry died in 1547.

Henry VIII first married on 11th June 1509, at Greenwich Palace, Kent. Katherine she was the daughter of Ferdinand V, King of Aragon, by Isabella I, Queen of Castile, a descendant of John of Gaunt, and she was born on 16th December 1485, at Alcala de Henares in Spain. She was crowned Queen Consort, on 24th June 1509, in Westminster Abbey. Thomas Cranmer Archbishop of Canterbury annulled her marriage to Henry VIII on 23rd May 1533, because she had been married to her husband's brother. She died, on 7th January 1536, at Kimbolton Castle, Hunts, supposedly of cancer, and she was buried in Peterborough Cathedral. Her original tomb was destroyed in 1642, but the site may still be seen, and her body still lies beneath the flagstones.

Henry VIII married secondly in secret, on 25th January 1533, either at York Place, London, or Westminster Palace. Anne she was the daughter of Thomas Boleyn, first Earl of Wiltshire and Ormonde, by Elizabeth, daughter of Thomas Howard, second Duke of Norfolk. She was born between 1500/1501 at Blickling Hall, Norfolk. She was styled Lady Marquees of Pembroke in her own right on 1st September 1523, and she was crowned Queen Consort on 1st June 1533, in Westminster Abbey. Anne Boleyn was found guilty of high treason, on 15th May 1536 and was condemned to death in the Tower of London, and executed on 19th May 1536, on Tower green, in the Tower of London. Anne she was buried in the Royal Chapel of St Peter ad Vincula, within the Tower of London.

Henry VIII married thirdly on 30th May 1536, at Whitehall Palace, London. Jane she was the daughter of Sir John Seymour by Margaret, daughter of Sir Henry Wentworth of Nettlestead, Suffolk, and she was born between, 1509/1510, probably at Wulfhall in Savernake Forest, Wiltshire. She was never crowned. She died, on 24th October 1537, at Hampton Court Palace, in childbed, and she was buried in St George's

Chapel, Windsor. Henry VIII married fourthly on 6th January 1540, at Greenwich Palace Kent.

Anne she was the daughter of John III, Duke of Cleves, by Mary, daughter of William III, Duke of Julich and Berg, and she was born on 22nd September 1515, at Dusseldorf, Cleves, Germany. Her marriage to Henry was annulled on 9th July 1540, because there was no consummation, she died on 16th/17th July 1557, at Chelsea Old Palace, London, and was buried in Westminster Abbey. There was no issue.

Henry VIII married fifthly on 28th July 1540, at Oatlands Palace, Surrey. Katherine she was the daughter of Lord Edmund Howard by Jocasta or Joyce, Daughter of Sir Richard Culpeper, and she was born in 1525, (date not known) either at Lambeth in London, or at Horsham, Sussex, she was never crowned. Katherine, she was found guilty of high treason, and executed, on 13th February 1542, on Tower Green in the Tower of London. She was buried in the Royal Chapel of St Peter ad Vincula. There was no issue.

Henry VIII married sixthly on 12th July 1543, at Hampton Court Palace. Katherine she was the daughter of Thomas Parr by Maud, daughter of Sir Thomas Green of Greens Norton, Northants, and she was born between 1512/1514, either at Kendal Castle, Westmoreland, or at her Fathers house at Blackfriars, London. After the death of Henry VIII, she married fourthly in April, or May 1547, Queen Jane's brother Thomas Seymour, 1st Baron Sudely. The other two marriages were, firstly Edward de Burgh, 2nd Baron Borough, secondly, John Neville 3rd Baron Latimer. She died on 7th September 1548, at Sudely Castle, Gloucester's, in childbed, and she was buried in Sudely Castle Chapel.

Henry VIII died on 28th January 1547, at Whitehall Palace, London, and he was buried in St George's Chapel, Windsor. His son Edward succeeded him, from his third marriage.

Edward VI

He was born on 12th October 1537, at Hampton Court Palace, Surrey, and he was duke of Cornwall from birth. He succeeded his father (age 9) as king of England on 28th January 1547, and was crowned on 20th/25th February 1547, in Westminster Abbey.

Upon the death of his father, Henry VIII, a regency was created, Although he was an intellectual person, with an education befitting a King, (fluent in Greek and Latin) he kept a full journal of his reign, he was not, however, a physically fit type of person. Using the Regency to strengthen their own positions, his short reign was dominated by his nobles. The King's Council succumbed to existing factionalism. (A Council previously dominated by his father Henry). Edward's eldest uncle, Edward Seymour, Earl of Hertford and Duke of Somerset, became his Protector.

Being an able soldier, he led an expedition against the Scots, because they failed to fulfil their promise to betroth Mary, Queen of Scots to him. In 1547, Edward Seymour was victorious at the Battle of Pinkie Cleugh, but he failed to follow this up with a satisfactory peace treaty. Edward himself was fiercely Protestant and the Church of England became more explicitly so. In 1549, the Book of Common Prayer was introduced an aspect of Roman Catholic practices was eradicated, and the marriage of clergy was introduced.

The imposition of the Prayer Book replacing Latin services with English, led to rebellions in Devon and Cornwall. In 1551, the Duke of Northumberland overthrew Seymour, because he was too liberal to deal with Kett's rebellion against land enclosures in Norfolk. In 1552, Seymour was executed by having his head cut off on Tower Hill. When Edward was found to be dying, Northumberland hurriedly married his son Lord Guilford Dudley, to Lady Jane Grey.

Edward VI died unmarried and childless, on 6th July 1553, at Greenwich Palace, Kent, and he was buried in Westminster Abbey. His second cousin Lady Jane Grey succeeded him.

Queen Jane

She was born in October 1537, at Bradgate Manor, Leicester. The Will of Henry VIII left the crown, in order of succession, to his children, Edward, Mary and Elizabeth, and then, if their line failed, to the heirs of his sister Mary, Duchess of Suffolk. When Edward VI died, he willed the crown to Jane, bypassing her mother Frances, who was rightful Queen after Mary and Elizabeth. Jane was proclaimed Queen of England, on 10th July 1553, but she only reigned for nine days because the People of England rallied to the cause of Mary Tudor. Jane the usurper was deposed, on 19th July 1553.

Duke of Northumberland, President of the King's Council, engineered the accession of Lady Jane Grey, in the interests of promoting his own dynastic line. When Northumberland herd that Edward VI was dying, he persuaded him to name Lady Jane Grey as his heir. Jane she was a genuine claimant to the throne, being one of Henry VIII great-nieces. Lord Guilford Dudley, Northumberland son, became Lady Jane's second husband.

Queen Jane married on 21st May 1553, either at Ely Place, Holborn, London, or at Durham House, Strand, London, it was not recorded as to where.

Guilford he was the son of John Dudley, Duke of Northumberland, by Jane, daughter of Sir Edward Guilford, and he was born in 1536, (date not recorded), he was executed on 12th February 1554, in Tower Hill, London, and was buried in the Royal Chapel of St Peter ad Vancula in the Tower of London. There was no issue.

Queen Jane was executed on 12th February 1554, (the same day has her husband), on Tower Green, in the Tower of London, and she was buried in the Royal Chapel of St Peter ad Vincula, within the Tower of London. Her second Cousin Mary had already succeeded her.

Mary I

She was born on 18th February 1516, at Greenwich Palace, Kent, and was proclaimed Queen of England upon the death of Queen Jane on 19th July 1553, although her regional years were dated from 24th July, she was crowned on 1st October 1553, at Westminster Abbey. She assumed the title Queen of Spain upon the accession of her husband Philip II, and to the throne of Spain, on 16th January 1556.

Mary I was a queen that reined in her own right, rather than a queen through marriage to a king, hence the title Queen Regnant. Mary she was the first Queen Regnant. In 1533, an Act of Parliament declared her illegitimate, and removed her from the succession, but she was reinstated in 1544. Mary was removed a second time by her half-brother Edward shortly before he died.

Mary abandoned the title of Supreme Head of the Church, and restored papal supremacy in England. She began the reintroduction of monastic orders by reintroducing Roman Catholic bishops. To secure the religious conversion of the country, Mary revived the old heresy laws, which could amount to treason, as a result, as many as 300 Protestant heretics, were burnt in three years. This made Mary very unpopular, but it demonstrated that people were prepared to die for the Protestant settlement.

In 1558, Calais was recaptured, when Spain dragged England into a war with France, Calais being the last vestige of England's possessions in France, dating from the time of William the Conqueror.

Mary I married on 25th July 1554, at Westminster Cathedral. Philip he was the son of Charles V, Holy Roman Emperor and king of Spain, by Isabella, daughter of Manuel I, King of Portugal, and he was born on 21st May 1527, at Valladolid, Spain. He became King of Portugal in 1580, he died on 13th September 1598, at the Palace of the Escarole, Madrid, Spain, and he was buried there, in the mausoleum.

Mary I died on 17th November 1558, at St James's Palace London, and she was buried in Westminster Abbey. Her half sister Elizabeth succeeded her.

Elizabeth I

She was born on 7th September 1533, at Greenwich Palace, Kent. She succeeded her half sister Mary I as Queen of England on 17th November 1558, and was crowned on 15th January 1559, at Westminster Abbey. Elizabeth was the daughter of Henry VIII, by Anne Boleyn. In 1537, when her half-brother Edward was born, the chances of Elizabeth succeeding to the throne must have seemed very slight, with her being only third in line.

In 1554, a rebellion against Queen Mary failed, Elizabeth she narrowly escaped execution, Fluent in six languages, very well educated, (Inherited probably from both parents) was her determination, intelligence, and shrewdness, and in English history, her 45-year reign was considered one of the most glorious. England also established a secure Church during her reign, and most likely saved England from religious wars like those the French suffered in the later half of the 16th century.

Elizabeth's astute political judgement helped her choose her ministers well, ministers like Walsingham, Secretary of State, and head of intelligence. Burghley also Secretary of State, and Hatton Lord Chancellor; in all some 600 officials administered the great offices of state, and a similar number dealt with the Crown lands, which funded the administrative costs.

Law and order remained in the hands of the sheriffs. Elizabeth witnessed many voyages of discovery, like those of Humphrey Gilbert, Walter Raleigh and Sir Francis Drake. During Elizabeth's reign the arts flourished, miniature paintings was the height of the day, theatres thrived,' and the first performance of A Midsummer Night's Dream' by Shakespeare was attended by Elizabeth herself. By buying expensive clothes and jewellery, she cultivated an image by touring the country in visits known as 'progresses, and during her reign she made at least 25.

Threats of invasion put Elizabeth, and many more in considerable danger, threats such as invasion's from Spain through Ireland, and from France through Scotland. In 1569/1570, most of northern England was in rebellion, and after plots against her life were discovered, (Roman Catholics considered her illegitimate). She passed sum very harsh laws against the Roman Catholics. One of the plots involved Mary, Queen of Scots, who in 1568, fled to England after her second husband's murder; her first husband Philip is thought to have been the instigator of the murder.

After the Babington Plot of 1586, Elizabeth saw Mary as a focus for possible rebellion and assassination plots; she was also a temptation for potential invaders such as Philip II. Seeing this Elizabeth kept her a prisoner: a prisoner for 19 years. In 1587, Mary was found guilty of treason and executed. Through his marriage to Mary, Philip II believed he had a claim to the throne of England. In 1588, with his 130 ships (known as the Armada) he invaded England, and by right of conquest Philip intended to re-establish Roman Catholicism, and overthrow the Queen, however the English navy fought back and England came out victorious.

Elizabeth the 'Virgin Queen' chose never to marry, being a selfless woman, she sacrificed her own happiness for the good of the nation, and when necessary she could be a very shrewd and decisive person. Both at home and abroad, her leadership brought successes during times of great danger. Elizabeth died in 1603, and for the next two hundred years, her accession was a national holiday.

Elizabeth I died on 24th March 1603, at Richmond Palace, Surrey, and she was buried in Westminster Abbey. Elizabeth was the last of the Tudor monarchs. Her third cousin, James VI of Scotland, succeeded her.

The Kings and Queens of Scotland From the 9th century to 1603

Time to retrace our steps chronologically through history to the 9th century, when the Kingdom of Scotland was first Founded. Before this date, details of the early rulers of Scotland are not very clear. The Scottish monarchy were probably the founder of the House of MacAlpine, which provided Scotland with Kings until the year 1034, when the succession passed to the House of Dunkeld via the marriage of Bethoc, daughter of Malcolm II, the House of Dunkeld then held sovereignty until the year 1290.

When Queen Margaret, (the Maid of Norway), died at sea, her death led to a bitter conflict for the throne, with thirteen competitors all eagerly waiting to claim the crown. Edward I of England was asked to choose, and he chose John Balliot. The Scots resented Edward's interference in their government, and Balliol was given no choice but to abdicate in 1296: thus followed the second Interregnum, which left Scotland without a King for the next ten years.

Edward I was then making great efforts to bring Scotland under English rule, until Robert le Bruce, declared himself King of Scotland in defiance of Edward in 1306. They say he was one of the Scots finest rulers. Bruce's dynasty did not survive very long, because his son died in 1371. The throne then passed to Bruce's grandson Robert II, son of Marjorie Bruce by Walter the Steward, who gave his name to the House of Stewart. The Stewart's then ruled Scotland for over two hundred years, and Great Britain for another one hundred years.

Part one: The house of Mac alpine

Up to the end of the eleventh century, other than their accession dates, little is known about many of the early kings of Scotland. Scotland at one time was occupied by five different types of people, the Picts in the north of the rivers Clyde. (A vast area) The Scots, from Ireland, occupied Argyll, in the fifth and sixth centuries. The Angles occupied and held Lothian. The ancient Britons had to retreat to Strathclyde, and the Norsemen lived in Orkney, Shetland, Caithness, Sutherland and the Western Isles.

It was not until the mid-ninth century when Kenneth MacAlpin became king, that unification of these different peoples began and perhaps the best-known Scottish island is the island of Iona the burial ground of many Scottish, Irish and Norwegian kings.

King Alpin

He succeeded his father as a King of Scotland, and became King of Kintyre in March/August 834, making him king of both Picts and Scots, thus he established his power over a wide area of Scotland; there are no records of any coronation.

King Alpin married a Scottish princess, whose name is unknown. King Alpin died on 20th July, or 20th August 834, whilst fighting the Picts in Galloway. His place of burial was not recorded. His son Kenneth succeeded him.

Kenneth I

He was the son of Alpin, King of Scotia, he succeeded his father as King of Galloway and other parts of Scotland on 20ᵗʰ July, or 20ᵗʰ August 843, and became King of the area known as DaLriada in 841. Sometime between 843/844, he defeated the Picts, uniting them with the Scots in the new kingdom of Alba, which comprised a large part of present day Scotland. Moreover, by 846, he was firmly established as King of Scotland; there are no records of his coronation.

The exact date of his victory over the Picts is unknown, but Kenneth was known to have been a very notable warrior, who is said to have invaded Northumbria six times, fought off attacks by the Britons of Strathclyde, and also fought of attacks by the Norsemen. To solve the problem off the attacks he married his daughter to Rhun, the Strathclyde king, because of the Norse threat to Iona, which was the burial place of St Columba; St Columba, being an Irish Scot who brought Christianity to Alba.

The new church which he founded in Pictland at Dunkeld, Perthshire, is where he removed all the saint's relics to, even after the removal off the relics, Iona continued to be the burial place of the Scottish kings, right up until the eleventh century.

Kenneth I married a Lady about whom no information exists, there are no records. Kenneth I died between 858/859, at Forteviot, near Perthshire, probably of a tumour, and he was buried on the Isle of Iona. His brother Donald succeeded him.

Donald I

He succeeded Kenneth I in 858/859, as king of Scotland. He died either in 863, in battle at Scone, Perthshire, or in his palace at Kinn Belachoir, very little his known about his brief reign, there are no records of any coronation. Donald I died unmarried and childless, his place of burial was never recorded. His nephew Constantine succeeded him.

Constantine I

He was the son of Kenneth I, and he succeeded Donald I as King of Scotland in 863. Constantine I married a Lady about whom no information exists. Constantine I was killed in 877, in battle against the Danes (known as the Norse), who invaded his kingdom several times, at Inverdorat, the Black Cove, Angus, and he was buried on the Isle of Iona. His brother Aedh succeeded him.

King Aedh

Another son of Kenneth I, he succeeded Constantine I as King of Scotland in 877, there are no records of any coronation. King Aedh married a Lady about whom no information exists, there are no records.

King Aedh was killed in 878, at Strathallan by Giric, who seized the throne for himself, and was probably buried at Maiden Stone, Aberdeenshire, The father of Giric is disputed; most historians claim that his father was a man called Dungal, who seems to have ruled jointly with Eochaid, who does not appear on the early lists of kings, but had some claim to the Pictish throne. Giric invaded Northumbria at least once. He died at Dundurn, in Perthshire, in 889. His nephew Eochaid succeeded him.

King Eochaid

He succeeded his father as King of Strathclyde, before succeeding his uncle, King Aedh as King of Scotland in 878, there are no records of any coronation, King Eochaid died unmarried and childless that same year. His place of burial was not recorded. His cousin Donald succeeded him.

Donald II

He was the Son of Constantine I; he succeeded his cousin Eochaid as King of Scotland in 889, there are no records of any coronation.

Donald II married a Lady about whom no information exists, there are no records. Donald II struggled to repel the Norse invasions, he was killed in 900, at Dun-forth, and he was buried on the Isle of Iona. His cousin Constantine succeeded him.

Constantine II

He was the son of Aedh; he succeeded Donald II as King of Scotland in 900. Constantine he ruled for over 40 years, repelling Norse raids and launching a series of invasions of Northumbria, in an attempt to establish a more stable relationship with the Norsemen of Ireland. Constantine married his daughter to Olaf III Guthfrithsson in the 930s, this dynastic marriage may have also intended to check the advance of Wessex, in northern England, if so, it failed.

Constantine was finally defeated in 937 by the Anglo-Saxon king Athelstan at the Battle of Brunanburh, where his eldest son was killed. He abdicated in 943, entered a Culdee monastery in St Andrews, Fife, where he later became Abbot. There are no records of any coronation.

Constantine II married a Lady about whom no information exists. Constantine II died at St Andrews Fife, in 952, and he was probably, buried there. His second cousin Malcolm succeeded him.

Malcolm I

He was the son of Donald II, he may have supported the establishment of a Danish kingdom of York in the 940s. He succeeded Constantine II as King of Scotland, between 942/943; there are no records of any coronation.

Malcolm I married a Lady about whom no information exists; there are no records, but he did have two sons King Duff, and Kenneth II, and one illegitimate son also named Kenneth.

Malcolm I he was killed in 954, possibly at Fetteresso, Kincardineshire by rebels from Moray, and he was buried on the Isle of Iona. His second cousin Indulf succeeded him.

King Indulf

He was the son of Constantine II, and he succeeded Malcolm I as King of Scotland in 954. King Indulf he abdicated in 962, and became a monk. It is said that Edinburgh passed to the Scots during his reign in 962; there are no records of any coronation.

King Indulf married a Lady, about whom no information exists; there are no records. King Indulf was killed the same year 962, by Viking invaders at the Battle of the Bauds, at the Muir of Findochty, Banffshire; his place of burial was not recorded, his third cousin Duff succeeded him.

King Duff

Alternatively, known as Dubh, and he was the son of Malcolm I who's Gaelic name means 'black'. He succeeded Indulf as King of Scotland in 962; there are no records of any coronation.

King duff married a Lady about no information exists; there are no records. King Duff was twice challenged for the throne, by King Colin, and on the second occasion he was killed in Moray, either in 966/967, at Forres, by the men of Moray. His place of burial was not recorded; his third cousin Colin succeeded him.

King Colin

Alternatively known as Culen, he was the son of Indulf, and he took the throne away by force from Dubh. He succeeded King Duff as King of Scotland in 967; there are no records of any coronation.

King Colin married a Lady about whom no information exists. King Colin he was killed in 971, by Riderch King of Strathclyde, whose daughter he had seized. His place of burial was not recorded. His third Cousin Kenneth succeeded him.

Kenneth II

He was the brother of Dubh; he succeeded King Colin as King of Scotland in 971. In 973, he acknowledged King Edgar of England has his lord in return for recognition that the Scots now held Lothian, which they had seized from the Angles. In about 994, however, he broke his promise to keep the peace and invaded England. He was defeated, and lost Lothian. Kenneth he killed Culen's brother in 977; there are no records of any coronation.

Kenneth II is said to have married a Princess, whose name is unknown, and had issue, Malcolm II, and Dungal his brother, who was murdered, by his own cousin Gillacomgain, son of Kenneth III in 999. Kenneth II was killed in 995, at Finella's Castle, Fettercairn. Kincardineshire by Culen's son, Constantine, in a blood feud, and he was buried on the Isle of Iona. His fourth cousin Constantine succeeded him.

Constantine III

He succeeded Kenneth II as King of Scotland in 995. Having killed Kenneth II; Constantine, son of Culen, made himself king. His reign was brief; there are no records of any coronation.

Constantine III married a Lady about whom no information exists. Constantine III was killed in 997, probably by Kenneth III, at Rathinveramon. There was no issue. His place of burial was not recorded; his fourth cousin Kenneth succeeded him.

Kenneth III

He was the son of Dubh; he succeeded Constantine III as King of Scotland in 997, According to one account; he tried to ensure that his own son Giric would succeed him, by making him joint king. However, Malcolm may have subsequently arranged the murder of Kenneth III's grandson, to enable a clear succession for his own grandson, Duncan I; there are no records of any coronation Kenneth III married a Lady about whom no information exists; there are no records. Kenneth III was killed on 25th March 1005, at the Battle of Monzievaird, Perthshire by his kinsman Malcolm, who seized the throne. His place of burial was not recorded. His cousin Malcolm succeeded him.

Malcolm II

Son of Kenneth II, he was born in 954. When he was young, he was styled Prince of Cumbria. He succeeded his cousin Malcolm, son of King Duff, as King of Strathclyde, between 990/991, and ruled Strathclyde until 995, when he was deposed. He was restored again in 997, and he succeeded Kenneth III as King of Scotland on 25th March 1005.

In 1018, when Kenneth II marched south, he took advantage of the fact that the English were preoccupied with Danish raids, thus winning the Battle of Carham against the Angles, and thereby regaining Lothian. That made him the first effective ruler of the whole of Scotland. There are no records of him ever being crowned.

Malcolm II married a Lady whose name is unknown, she is thought to have been an Irishwoman from Ossory, but there are no records to prove this.

Malcolm II died (aged 80) on 25th November 1034, at Glamis Castle, Angus, mortally wounded by his kinsmen, and he was buried on the Isle of Iona. Malcolm he was the last sovereign of the House of MacAlpine. His grandson Duncan succeeded him.

Part two: the house of Dunkeld

Duncan I

Known as the Gracious, he was the son of Malcolm II's eldest daughter Bethoc, by her husband Crinan. (Lay Abbot of Dunkeld) He was about 33 when he succeeded his grandfather. Married to a cousin of Siward, Earl of Northumberland, he probably favoured southern ways, and this is why he became very unpopular with his subjects. Duncan he was born in 1001 and he became King of Strathclyde in 1018. He succeeded his grandfather, Malcolm II, as King of Scotland on 25th November 1034, that made him the first Sovereign of the House of Dunkeld, named after his father's abbacy. In 1039, Duncan marches south to besiege Durham but he was pushed back, with heavy losses, the Earl of Orkney's son, Thorfinn, then twice defeated him.

Malcolm was never crowned; there are no records of his coronation.

Duncan I married in 1030, but there are no records existing as to where. Sybilla she was either the daughter of Bjorn Bearsson and sister of Siward Digera, Earl of Northumbria, or the daughter of Siward by Elfleda, daughter of Ealdred, Earl of Northumbria. Nothing else is known; there are no records.

Duncan I was killed in battle by Macbeth, one of his commanders, on 14th August 1040, at Bothganowan, (now Pitgaveny), near Elgin Morayshire, and he was buried on Isle of Iona. His cousin Macbeth succeeded him.

King Macbeth

He was born in 1005. He became Mormaer of Moray between 1029/1032. (A Mormaer was literally a High Steward of one of the ancient Celtic provinces of Scotland). He succeeded Duncan I as King of Scotland on 14th August 1040. His reign was for the most part peaceful, and he was known for his generosity to the Church. He made a pilgrimage to Rome in 1050, and started 'scattering money like seed', for the people.

Macbeth he killed Duncan, who was about 39, in battle, and made himself king, and Macbeth's, marriage to Kenneth III's granddaughter Gruoch probably strengthened his claim to the throne. In 1045, Macbeth defeated and killed Duncan I's father Crinan at Dunkeld. Macbeth he was never crowned; there are no records of his coronation.

King Macbeth married shortly after 1032; but there are no records as to where.

Gruoch, she was the daughter of Beoedhe, son of Kenneth III. She was born in 1015; the date of her death is not known. There was no issue to this marriage.

King Macbeth was killed on 15th August 1057, at the Battle of Lumphanan, Aberdeenshire, by Duncan's eldest son, Malcolm Canmore, and he was buried on the Isle of Iona. His stepson Lulach succeeded him.

King Lulach

Known as "the simple", he was Macbeth's stepson, and the son of Gruoch by her first husband, Gillacomgan, Mormaer of Moray, and he was born between 1029/1032. He succeeded his stepfather Macbeth as King of Scotland on 15th August 1057, and he was crowned the same month, on the coronation Stone at Scone Abbey, Perthshire. This was the first time the crowning of a King of Scotland was recorded.

King Lulach married but on record exists has to when or where. Finnghuala she was the daughter of Sinill, Mormaer of Angus, nothing else is known about her, the dates have not been recorded.

King Lulach was killed on 17th March 1058, at Strathbogie by his distant cousin and successor, Malcolm III, and he was buried on the Isle of Iona. Malcolm, son of Duncan I succeeded him.

Malcolm III

Known as Malcolm "Canmore" (or "Bighead"), he was the eldest son of Duncan I. After his father's death, he found refuge in England with his uncle Siward of Northumbria, where he stayed for more than 14 years. Malcolm he was born in 1031 and he became King of Strathclyde and Prince of Cumbria in 1034. He succeeded Lulach as King of Scotland on 17th March 1058, and he was crowned on 25th April 1058, at Scone Abbey, Perthshire.

His first wife was Ingibiorg, when she died he married Margaret, who sought refuge in Scotland with her brother, Edgar the Atheling (Anglo-Saxon heir to the English throne), when William I excluded Malcolm from the English succession. Margaret had a strong influence over her husband; he secretly had jewel-encrusted bindings made for her religious books, which he himself was unable to read.

He also substituted Saxon for Gaelic as the court language. According to Margaret's biographer, she corresponded with Lanfranc, Archbishop of Canterbury, brought Benedictine monks to Dunfermline and did away with local usages in the Scottish Church. Margaret also began building, St Margaret's Chapel, situated on the highest part of Edinburgh Castle.

Malcolm was defeated in battle three times, and was forced under the treaty of Abernethy in 1072, to become 'the man' of the English king, and give up his son Duncan as a hostage. His wife died when they brought her the news at Edinburgh Castle. After Malcolm's death, the frontier between the kingdoms of Scotland and England, were clearly defined for the first time. Anglo- Norman influence in Scotland was promoted by the subsequent marriages of Malcolm's son's to English brides.

Malcolm III first married either in 1059 or 1066, but there are no records as to where. Ingibiorg she was the daughter of Finn Arnasson of Vrjar, Jarl, of Holland, by Bergljot, daughter of Halfdan Sigurdsson, and she was the widow of Earl Thorfinn of Orkney. The date of her birth is not known. She died between 1069/1070.

Malcolm III married secondly in 1069, at Dunfermline Abbey, Fife. St Margaret she was the daughter of Edward the Atheling, son of Edmund II, King of England, by Agatha of Hungary, and she was also the great-niece of King Edward the Confessor, King of England. She was born between 1045/1046, in Hungary. She died, on 16th November 1093, at Edinburgh Castle, and she was buried in Dunfermline Abbey Fife; her remains were later transported to the Escorial Madrid, Spain, her head being buried in the Jesuit College at Douai, France. She was canonised as a saint between 1249/1250.

Malcolm III was killed (aged about 62) along with his eldest son, on 13th November 1093, in battle near Alnwick, Northumberland, and he was buried at Tynemouth, his remains were later removed to Dunfermline Abbey, Fife, and later still to the Escorial Madrid, Spain. His brother Donald succeeded him.

Donald III

Known as "Donald bane", he was the younger brother of Malcolm III, and he was born in 1033. He succeeded his brother in 1093, at the age of 60, and was thought to have been created Mormaer or Earl of Gowrie in 1060. He usurped the throne of Scotland, on 13th November 1093, upon the death of his brother Malcolm III: but was deposed by Malcolm's son Duncan II in May 1094, with the assistance of William II (Rufus) of England. When Duncan II died, Donald III was restored to the throne as joint monarch, with his nephew King Edmund, Donald ruling north of the Forth/Clyde line, "Scotia", and Edmund ruling south of it, "Lothian and Strathclyde". Both Donald and Edmund were deposed in favour of King Edgar in October 1097. No record exists of Donald ever being crowned.

At the start of the twelfth century, Scotland saw a religious revival and improved administration under David I, the most successful of Malcolm Canmore's sons to become king. He organised the building of the great Border abbeys, the granting of town charters, and the first standard coinage. In this period and subsequently, the close relationship of Scottish kings with the English court, often reinforced by marriage, led to the expansion of English as the language of government, and the rise of Anglo-Norman aristocracy in Scotland.

Quarrels among Scottish nobles, at the end of the thirteenth century, about who should inherit the throne after the death of Alexander III, led to King Edward I of England's aggressive intervention, and the Wars of Independence. William Wallace led the struggle for Scottish independence from England in 1297, he won the battle against the English at Stirling Bridge, but the conflict with England was not over yet, it lasted on and off for the next 300 years.

Donald III married a Lady about whom no information exists, but they did have a daughter named Bethoc.

Donald III died in 1099, accounts of his fate differ, according to one version, he was blinded and kept prisoner until his death at Rescobie Angus, another account was that he was ultimately executed in London. Donald was buried in Dunkeld Abbey; his remains were later removed to the Isle of Iona. He was the last Scottish king to be buried on Iona. King Edgar succeeded him.

Duncan II

He was the eldest son of Malcolm III by his first wife Ingibiorg; he was born in 1060. Duncan spent 15 years as a hostage in England before being released by William II in 1087. When he deposed his uncle, Donald III, he proclaimed himself King of Scotland in May 1094. Duncan's now personal relationship with England made him very unpopular in Scotland, because effectively he had become an English vassal; there are no records of his coronation.

Duncan II married between 1090/1094, no records exists as to where. Ethelreda or Octreda she was the daughter of Gospatrick, Earl of Northumbria, and Unbar, a great-grandson of Malcolm II, there are no records of her date of birth or death, she was buried in Dunfermline Abbey Fife.

Duncan II was killed on 12th November 1094, at the Battle of Monthechin (Mondynes), Kincardineshire, by the Mormaer of the Mearns, and he was buried in Dunfermline Abbey, Fife. Donald III succeeded him, the man he had deposed.

King Edmund

He was styled Prince of Cumbria, when he was only a very young boy. He became joint King of Scotland with Donald III, his uncle on 12th November 1094. Following the death of his half brother, Duncan II, Edmund's authority was limited to the area south of the Forth/Clyde line, while Donald III ruled the North of the Forth/Clyde. King Edmund, and Donald III, was deposed in October 1097, in favour of his brother Edgar. Edmund was never crowned; there are no records of his coronation.

King Edmund became a monk at Montacute Abbey, Somerset, where he later died, the date of his death is not known. He was probably buried in Montacute Abbey. He never married, and never had issue. He was succeeded by his Brother Edgar.

King Edgar

He was the fourth son of Malcolm III, and he was born between 1073/1074. He succeeded Donald III and King Edmund (joint rulers) as King of Scotland in October 1097. In 1095, William II of England recognised him as the rightful King of Scotland. In return, Edgar agreed to hold Scotland as William's vassal. The following year, an English army helped Edgar to seize the throne from his uncle, Donald III. In 1100, his sister Matilda (Maud) married Henry I of England and so he became the English king's brother-in- law. Edgar he was never crowned; there is no record of his Coronation.

Edgar's submissive attitude to England: and his presentation of the Western Isles to the king of Norway, led to what could be called his insulting nickname 'the Peaceable'.

King Edgar he himself did not marry, he died unmarried and childless on 8th January 1107, (aged about 33) either at Dundee, or at Edinburgh Castle, (the later is more likely), and he was buried in Dunfermline Abbey, Fife. His brother Alexander succeeded him.

Alexander I

Known as "the fierce", he was born between 1077/1078. He succeeded his brother Edgar as King of Scotland, on 8th January 1107. Alexander was the fifth son of Malcolm III by St Margaret, named after Pope Alexander II. One chronicler described him as 'a lettered and godly man. He was never crowned; there are records of his coronation.

Alexander became known as the Fierce' after dealing ruthlessly with an uprising in Moray, and in 1114, he served as leader in Henry I of England's military campaign against the Welsh.

Alexander I married in 1107, but there are no records as to where. Sybilla she was an illegitimate daughter of Henry I King of England, by Sybille Cornet, and she was, born in 1092 at Domfront, Normandy. She died suddenly on 12th/13th July 1122, on the Island of the Woman, Loch Tay, Perthshire, and was probably, buried in a church there; there was no issue. Alexander I died on 23rd of April 1124, at Stirling Castle, and he was buried in Dunfermline Abbey, Fife. His brother David succeeded him.

David I

He was the sixth and youngest son of Malcolm III, by St Margaret. He was born between 1080/1081, and was designated Prince of Cumbria in 1107. He was styled Earl of Huntingdon in right of his wife, from 1113/1114: and he held the Earldom of Northampton, and the Honour of Huntingdon, with a legitimate claim to a substantial part of England. He succeeded his brother Alexander as King of Scotland either on 23rd/24th or 27th April 1124.

He was by then in his mid-40s, and was famous for his piety. Indeed, he was later criticised as being 'a sair sanct for the crown, but he was never crowned; there are no records of his coronation. David he was a gentle, just, and humble ruler, loved for his gentleness, feared for his justice, and he was known as "the saint", and was always remembered as one after his death.

David I married between 1113/1114; there are no records as to where. Matilda she was the daughter of Waltheof, Earl of Huntingdon and Northampton, by Judith, daughter of Lambert of Boulogne, Count of Lens, by Adeline, sister of William I, king of England, and she was born in 1074. She died between 1130/1131, and she was buried in Scone Abbey, Perthshire.

David I died on 24th May 1153, at Carlisle in Cumbria, (aged about 73) and he was buried in Dunfermline Abbey, Fife, where he had extended the church into an abbey in commemoration of his parents. His grandson Malcolm succeeded him.

Malcolm IV

Known as "the Maiden", he was born between 1141/1142. He succeeded his grandfather David I (at the age of 12) as King of Scotland on 24th May 1153, and was crowned soon afterwards, at Scone Abbey, Perthshire, (date unknown). Malcolm's succession to the throne as a minor caused problem in 1157, he conceded Cumberland and Westmoreland to Henry II in exchange for the Earldom of Huntingdon, but there is no suggestion he compromised his kingship by doing so in any way.

The leading men of his kingdom resented the Anglo-Norman ways of his grandfather David I, so Malcolm went to France in 1159 with Henry II of England, and was present at the siege of Toulouse. On his return home to Perth Castle, he was besieged by six of his Earls, with the intervention of clergy, the king and his nobles were reconciled. Malcolm his homage to Henry II in 1163 led to further rebellions by the earls in 1164.

Malcolm IV died unmarried and childless on 9th December 1165, at Jedburgh Castle (at the age of 23) and he was buried beside his grandfather in front of the high altar in the Church of the Holy Trinity, Dunfermline Abbey Fife. His brother William succeeded him.

King William

Known as "the Lion", he was the younger brother of Malcolm IV; he was born between 1142/1143. He succeeded his father as Earl of Northumberland on 12th June 1152, but he gave up this earldom in 1157. He succeeded Malcolm IV as King of Scotland on 9th December

1165, and he was crowned on 24th December 1165, at Scone Abbey, Perthshire.

In June 1153, a year after his accession, he went to Normandy with Henry II, and later spent Easter in 1170, at Windsor. In 1174, he invaded England, when he joined Henry II's son in his rebellion against his father, but he was captured at Alnwick, Northumberland, and brought to Henry II, with his feet securely chained beneath the belly of his horse; Henry then held him a prisoner, first in Yorkshire, then at Northampton, and finally in France. He was finally released by the terms of the Treaty of Falaise on 8th December 1174, having agreed to do homage to Henry II 'for Scotland, and for all other parts of his lands'; he also had to surrender key Scottish castles such as Edinburgh castle and Stirling castle.

Henry now had the right, as William's feudal lord, to arrange his marriage to Ermengarde de Beaumont, whose father was the son of an illegitimate daughter of Henry I, however William recovered Scotland from Henry II's feudality, and when Richard I succeeded Henry II, he was determined to raise money for his third Crusade. Therefore, he surrendered his feudality over Scotland for 10,000 marks by the Quitclaim of Canterbury on 5th December 1189, and Scotland became an independent country once more.

Under William, the development of feudal institutions continued; in part, the Scottish monarchy's government, closely resembled England's. William he established royal burghs in eastern Scotland up to the Moray Firth, and extended the use of sheriffs in the same area. Perth and Stirling then became major centres of royal administration.

William I married on 5th September 1186, at Woodstock Palace Oxon. Ermengarde she was the daughter of Richard, Viscount of Beaumont-le- Maine, by Constance, illegitimate daughter of Henry I King of England. There are no records of her date of birth. She died on 11th February either in 1233/1234, and she was buried in Balmerino Abbey, Fife.

King William I died on 4th December 1214, at Stirling, and he was buried in Arbroath Abbey, Scotland, (aged 71). He was succeeded by his son Alexander.

Alexander II

He was born on 24th August 1198, at Haddington, East Lothian. He succeeded his father as King of Scotland on 4th December 1214, and was crowned on 6th December 1214, at Scone Abbey, Perthshire. Alexander was the only son of William the Lyon, by his wife Ermengarde, who was born at Haddington, East Lothian on 24th August 1198; King John of England knighted Alexander on 4th March 1212. Two years later, he succeeded his father, although Alexander backed the barons who forced John to sign the Magna Carta.

In 1237, the long-standing dispute between Scotland and England over its borders was settled, and in exchange for the honour of Tynedale and the manor of Penrith, Alexander renounced Scotland's claims to the three northern counties of England. The border between England, and Scotland, was now fixed on its present line; from the Solway Firth in the west, to the lower Tweed in the east, and it remains, almost the same to day.

Alexander II first married on 18th/25th June 1221, at York Minster. Joan she was the eldest daughter of John, King of England, by Isabelle of Angouleme, and she was born on 22nd July 1210, or the 22nd July 1203 in Normandy. She died either on 4th/5th or the 12th March 1238, at Havering- atte-Bower, Essex, and she was buried in Torrent Crowford Abbey, Dorset. There was no issue.

Alexander II married secondly on 15th May 1239, at Roxburgh. Mary she was the daughter of Enguerrand III, Baron de Coucy Lord of Couch, by Mary, Daughter of John, Lord of Montmirel-en-Brie, an alliance, which raised English fears of a Franco-Scottish alliance, and she was buried at Newbottle, Scotland; the date of her death was not recorded.

Alexander II died on 6th July 1249, on the Isle of Kerrara Argyllshire in the Bay of Oban, whilst preparing to take the Hebrides from Norway, and he was buried in Melrose Abbey, Roxburghshire. His son Alexander, from his second marriage succeeded him.

Alexander III

Known as "the glorious", he was born on 4th September 1241, at Roxburgh. He was the only son of Alexander II, by his second wife, Marie de Coucy. He succeeded his father as King of Scotland, on 8th July 1249, and he was crowned on 13th July 1249, at Scone Abbey, Perthshire. Alexander became king at the age of seven, on the death of his father. On Christmas Day 1251, at the age of ten, Henry III knighted him at York, and the following day he was married to the English monarch's eldest daughter.

In 1263 his army inflicted a remarkable defeat on Hakon, King of Norway, at the Battle of Largs in Ayrshire, and in 1266, the Norwegians were forced to concede to him (under the treaty of Perth), the Western Isles and the Isle of Man. When Alexander and his brother-in-law Edward I, first met they established good relations with each other. On 19th August 1274, Alexander and Margaret attended the coronation of her brother in Westminster Abbey, but sadly, Margaret died six months later. Within the next a few years, he suffered further family loses. At the age of eight in 1281, his younger son David died. In 1283, his daughter Margaret, who had married King Eric of Norway, died in childbirth, and in 1284, after a long illness, his elder son Alexander died childless. Alexander was 44 when he married his second wife Yolanda.

Alexander III first married on 26th December 1251, at York Minster. Princess Margaret she was the daughter of Henry III, King of England, by Eleanor of Provence, and she was born on 29th September, or 5th October 1275, at Cupar Castle, Fife, and was buried in Dunfermline Abbey, Fife, leaving three children.

Alexander III married secondly on 1st November 1285, at Jedburgh Abbey. Yolanda Countess de Montfort, she was the daughter of Robert IV, Count of Dreux, there are no records of her date of birth. She died in 1323. There was no issue.

Alexander III was killed on 19th March 1286, when his horse stumbled and he fell from a cliff, somewhere between Burntisland and Kinghorn, Fife, leaving the Scots to mourn an energetic, effective monarch who had brought them peace and prosperity; he was buried in Dunfermline Abbey Fife. His Granddaughter Margaret succeeded him.

Queen Margaret

Known as "the Maid of Norway", she was born on 9th April 1283, or may be shortly before, somewhere in Tonsberg, Norway. She succeeded her grandfather Alexander III on 19th March 1286, has Scotland's first ever Queen Regnant. When her grandfather died, Princess Margaret, 'the Maid of Norway', was only three years old. The Scottish Parliament appointed six Guardians to rule on her behalf, and on 18th July 1290, the Scots agreed (in the Treaty of Birgham Berwickshire) that she should marry Edward I of England's eldest son, Prince Edward. Margaret was never crowned; there are no records of her coronation.

Queen Margaret died in either May 1290, or 26th September 1290, on board a ship, on her way to Scotland. Margaret became ill on the voyage, and her ship put in at Orkney, but she died there, in the arms of the Bishop. Her body was taken back to Bergen, Norway, where she was buried beside her mother.

When the Maid of Norway died, it left Scotland without a monarch, and at the mercy of Edward I of England. In 1290 began the first Interregnum: and a contest for the throne began between 13 Competitors. The thirteen claimants were then reduced to three: John Balliol, Robert Bruce, and John Hastings, all of whom were descendants of the three daughters of David, Earl of Huntingdon. From these, Edward I was asked to choose which had the most lawful claim to the crown, and he Chose John Balliol as Scotland's next king.

Part three: the house of Balliot

King John

He was the son of John, fifth Baron de Balliol by his wife Devorgilla, daughter of Alan, Lord of Galloway. He was born between 1249/1250, His nickname, "Toom Tabard" or ("Tern coat"), is thought to have referred to the ceremonious removal of heraldic insignia from his coat, as part of his submission. John he was created Baron, of Bywell in Northumberland: but he forfeited this honour in 1285. Edward I of England awarded him the crown of Scotland at Berwick, on 17th November 1292, thus bringing to an end the First interregnum.

John was crowned on 30th November 1292, at Scone Abbey, Perthshire, but he abdicated on 10th/11th July 1296 at Brechin Scotland. That left Scotland without a King, thus bringing about the Second Interregnum, which Lasted until 1306, when Robert Bruce seized the throne in defiance of Edward I, who had tried during those 10 years to take it himself, and make Scotland a fief of England. Balliol finally renounced his fealty to Edward I on 5th April 1296.

Edward I marched north, defeated the Scots at the Battle of Dunbar in East Lothian, and captured the castles of Roxburgh, Edinburgh and Stirling. On 10 July 1296, Balliol surrendered himself, and his kingdom to Edward I of England. In 1296, Edward I marched north as far as Elgin, then south to Scone, and took the Stone of Destiny, on which the Scottish kings were crowned, and had it sent to Westminster Abbey, were it remained for the next 700 years: before England returned it to Scotland in 1996.

King John married in February, either in 1280 or 1281. There are no records as to where. Isabella she was the daughter of John de Warenne, 6th Earl of Surrey, by Alice, daughter of Hugh X de Lusignan, Count of La Marche, by Isabella of Angouleme, widow of King John, of England. Isabella was born in 1253; the date of her death was never recorded.

King John was taken to England as a prisoner, but in 1299, he was allowed passage to France where he lived on his family estates. He died on 4th March 1313/1314, at Bailleut-en-Gouffern, Normandy, (at the age of 63) and he was perhaps, buried in the Church of St Waast, Normandy. His son Robert succeeded him.

William Wallace, Guardian of Scotland

Most Scots continued to regard John Balliol as their rightful king. In 1297, William Wallace, son of Sir Malcolm Wallace of Elderslie, Renfrewshire, organised a revolt against England's occupation of Scotland, and after having killed the English sheriff of Lanark, led him to waged a highly successful guerilla warfare against the English, and gradually won back his kingdom. He then joined forces with Sir Andrew Moray on 11th September 1297, and routed the English at the Battle of Stirling Bridge. Now he could invade the north of England, once he had recaptured Berwick, and trade with the merchants of Lübeck and Hanover once more. William Wallace, he was knighted, and proclaimed Guardian of the realm, in the name of John Balliol.

Edward I of England continued to wage war against him, and Wallace was defeated at the Battle of Falkirk, Stirlingshire on 22nd July 1298. After the Battle of Falkirk, he resigned his Guardianship, and travelled to France in an unsuccessful attempt to enlist support. In 1305, Wallace was betrayed to the English, and he was captured near Glasgow, he was then taken to London, and on 23rd August 1305, he was hanged, drawn and quartered, after being tried for treason at Westminster Hall.

Part four: the house of Bruce

Robert I

Known as "the Bruce", he was born either in Ayr on 11th July 1274, or at Writtle, near Chelmsford, Essex. He was the son of Robert Bruce, Earl of Carrick, and the grandson of the Robert Bruce who had been one of the competitors for the throne after the death of the Maid of Norway. He succeeded his father as Earl of Carrick on 27th October 1292; and as Lord of Annandale, either in 1295 or 1304. He assumed the monarchy and Royal Dignity of Scotland, bringing to an end the second Interregnum.

This he did in defiance of Edward I of England, who had declared his English Estates forfeit on 20th February 1305/1306. After the death of William Wallace, Robert the Bruce took up the struggle for Scotland's independence, and he was crowned King of Scotland, on 27th March 1306, at Scone Abbey, Perthshire. His reign did not get of to a very good start he was defeated by the English at Methven in Perthshire; his wife, daughter and sisters were imprisoned, and three of his brothers were executed by the English.

Robert I first married in 1295, there are no records as to where. Isabelle she was the daughter of Donald 6th Earl of Mar, by his wife Helen, who is thought to have been an illegitimate daughter of Llywelyn the Great, Prince of Wales. She died either in 1300/1302, date not recorded. Robert I married secondly in 1302, but there are no records existing as to where. Elizabeth she was the daughter of Richard de burgh, Earl of Ulster and Connaught, by Margaret, daughter of John de Burgh. Her date of birth was not recorded. She died, on 26th October

1372, at Cullen Castle, Banffshire, and was buried in Dunfermline Abbey, fife.

Robert I died on 7th June 1329, at Cardross Castle, Dumbartonshire, and he was buried in Dunfermline Abbey, Fife. His heart being carried back to the Holy Land, by Sir James, but Sir James was killed fighting the Moors in Granada, in Spain; the heart was retrieved though, and brought back to Scotland, where it was buried in Melrose Abbey, Roxburghshire. His son David, from his second marriage succeeded him.

David II

He was born on 5th March 1324, at Dunfermline Place, Fife. He was the elder and only surviving son of Robert I. He became Scotland's first anointed king on the death of his father. He was created Earl of Carrick, either on 17th March or 17th July 1328. (It has long been tradition that the title of Earl of Carrick as always gone to the eldest son of the sovereign in Scotland). David he succeeded his father as King of Scotland on 7th June 1329, and he was crowned on 24th November 1331, at Scone Abbey, Perthshire.

He was defeated by Edward Balliol in August 1332, at the Battle of Dupplin Moor, near Perth, but was restored to the throne the following December, he was again deposed by Edward Balliol in 1333, and finally restored in 1336. On 26th August 1346, Edward III defeated the French at the battle of Crecy. David II, now aged 17, decided to invade England in support of his ally, France, but he was defeated and captured at the Battle of Neville's Cross-, near Durham on 17th October 1346. David was held prisoner in the south for eleven years, during which time his nephew, Robert the Steward, ruled Scotland.

David II first married (at the age of only four) on 17th July 1328, at Berwick-upon-Tweed, Northumberland. Joan she was the daughter of Edward II, King of England, by Isabelle of France, and she was born on 5th July 1321, in the Tower of London. She was crowned Queen Consort, on 24th November 1331, at Scone Abbey, Perthshire. This was the first time a Scottish Queen Consort, as ever been crowned. In 1361, David tried unsuccessfully to divorce her when she failed to provide an heir, but Joan died suddenly on 7th September 1362, at Hertford Castle, and she was buried in Greyfriars, church, Newgate, London. There was no issue. David II married secondly either in April, December 1363, or 13th/20th February 1364, either at Inchmurdach Manor, Fife, or at Inchmahome Priory, Perthshire.

Margaret she was the daughter of Sir Malcolm Drummed by a daughter of Sir Patrick de Graham. David II divorced Margaret, on 20th March 1370. She died some five years later in January 1375, probably at Avignon, France. There was no issue to either of these marriages.

David II died on 22nd February 1371, at Edinburgh Castle, and he was buried in Hollyrood, Abbey Edinburgh. Edward III once said that if David did die childless, the King of England should succeed to the Scottish throne. The Scottish Parliament refused to ratify the proposals, and when David died childless in 1371, his nephew Robert Stewart succeeded him.

Continuation of part three:
The House of Balliol

King Edward Balliol

He was the elder son of John Balliol King of the Scots, his date of birth is unknown; he claimed the throne of Scotland as his father's successor. During the minority of David II, Balliol invaded Scotland with the help of the English, routed the Scots on 11th/12th August 1332, at the Battle of Dupplin Moor, near Perth, and he was crowned King of Scotland on 24th September 1332, at Scone Abbey, Perthshire. He was deposed in favour of David II on 16th December 1332, and expelled from Scotland, but was restored to the throne in March 1333, he was again deposed in 1334, and was forced to flee south, so he left for England, but he returned; held a parliament at Edinburgh and was restored once more in 1335. He was finally deposed in 1336. King Edward he gave up all claims to the throne of Scotland on 20th January 1356.

King Edward died unmarried and childless in January 1364, at Wheatley, near Doncaster, Yorkshire, (the place of his burial was not recorded). David II succeeded King Edward, in 1336, and in turn was succeeded by Robert Stewart.

Part five: the house of Stewart

Robert II

He was born on 2nd March 1316, at Paisley, Renfrewshire. He was the son of Robert I's daughter, Marjorie by her husband Walter the Steward. He succeeded David II, (at the age of 54) as King of Scotland (the first Stewart King) on 22nd February 1371, and was crowned on 22nd February, or 26th March 1371, at Scone Abbey, Perthshire. When he took the surname Stewart, he became the first monarch of the Royal House of Stewart. He was created Earl of Atoll on 16th February 1342, and he was created Earl of Strathearn, ether in 1357/1358, but he gave up the earldom of Atoll on 31st May 1367, and he resigned, or was deprived of the earldom of Strathearn on 18th April 1369. He was formally deprived of it on 16th September 1369, but he was restored in blood to the earldom of Strathearn on 4th/7th April 1370.

Robert II first married in 1336. There are no recorders as to where. Elizabeth she was the daughter of Sir Adam Moore of Rowan, Ayrshire, by Joan Cunningham, his wife, or Janet Moore, his second wife. The children of this marriage most of them being born before the second ceremony, were illegitimate, and the fact that his first wife's children were born outside the marriage created long-standing bitterness as Robert III's reign was to show, but one of his sons did succeed his father as King. Elizabeth, she died between 1354/1355. There are no records as to where. Robert II married secondly in May 1355. There are no records as to where.

Euphoria she was the daughter of Hugh, sixth Earl of Ross, by Margaret Graham. She was crowned Queen Consort in 1372, at Scone Abbey, Perthshire. She died in 1387.

Robert II Robert married twice, and produced 21 children (eight were illegitimate), During Robert II's final years his two eldest sons acted as his lieutenants. He died on 19th April 1390, at Dundonald Castle, Ayrshire, and he was buried in Scone Abbey, Perthshire. His son John, who took the name Robert upon his accession, succeeded him.

Robert III

He was succeeded by his 53-year-old son John; he was born between 1337/1340. He was created Earl of Carrick on 22nd June 1368, and he was made Earl of Atoll on 17th October 1379. He succeeded his father as King of Scotland on 19th April 1390. In addition, he was crowned, on 14th August 1390, at Scone Abbey, Perthshire. Robert he had to suffer from many disadvantages, he was born illegitimate (made legitimate in 1347), and not only that, he had been disabled in 1388 by a horse's kick, so he was regarded as unfit to govern for his father.

Robert he was dominated by his younger brother, the Duke of Albany, and when he tried to rule for himself; his misrule was condemned in 1399, by the Scottish Parliament, so his elder son David, Duke of Rothesay was appointed to govern for him. However, Albany, imprisoned his nephew and David died in mysterious circumstances in 1402, he is said to have been starved to death, or more probably he succumbed to dysentery.

Robert III married between 1366/1367. There are no records as to where. Annabelle she was the daughter of Sir John Drummond of Stobhall, by Mary, daughter of Sir William Montifex, and she was born in 1350. She was crowned Queen Consort on 15th August 1390, at Scone Abbey, Perthshire; She died in October 1401, at Scone Palace, Perthshire, and was buried in Dunfermline Abbey, Fife.

Robert III died on 4th April 1406, at Dundonald Castle, Ayrshire, soon after hearing that the 11-year-old prince, (his younger son James), who he had sent to France for safety, had been captured at sea by English pirates. He was buried in Paisley Abbey Renfrewshire. His son James succeeded him.

James I

He was born on 25th, in either July or December 1394, at Dunfermline Palace, Fife. He was created Duke of Rothesay and Earl of Carrick on 10th December 1404. He succeeded his father as King of Scotland on 4th April 1406, but he was not proclaimed until June, whilst being held in captivity by Henry IV of England, who saw that he received an appropriate education, fit for his royal birth.

James was intelligent and a cultivated monarch, who loved to write poetry, he loved music, and was a fine athlete. (He wrote the poem "The King's Quire") he was also determined to restore law and order in his kingdom - and it was James I who founded what was to become the Court of Session.

One day in 1423, looking out of his window, he saw a beautiful young woman, Lady Joan Beaufort, a close relative of the English king, Henry VI, and it was probably through her influence that the Treaty of London was agreed in December 1423. James was not released from his captivity, until January 1424. Releasing him for a ransom of £40,000, the couple were married the following February, and travelled north to be crowned either on the 2nd/21st May 1424, at Scone Abbey Perthshire.

James I married on 2nd/10th or 13th February 1424, at the Priory Church of St Mary Ovary, Southwark London. Joan she was the daughter of John Beaufort, Earl of Somerset, a grandson of Edward III, King of England, by Margaret Holland. She was crowned Queen Consort on 2nd/21st May 1424, at Scone Abbey, Perthshire. Joan died on 15th July 1445, at Dunbar Castle, and she was buried in the Monastery of the Charterhouse, Perth.

James I was assassinated, (and his queen badly injured), on 21st February 1437, by his Uncle Walter, Earl of Atholl, (a son from Robert II's; second marriage), in the monastery of the Dominican Friars in Perth. James was particularly determined to curb his rivals descended from Robert II; he arrested some and executed others (including the new Duke of Albany), and confiscated estates, the result, assassination. James he was buried in Perth, in the monastery of the Cartesians, which he had founded. His son James succeeded him.

James II

He was born on 16th October 1430, at Holyrood Palace, Edinburgh, (the younger of twins). He succeeded his brother Alexander as duke of Rothesay, in 1430. He succeeded his father as King of Scotland on 21st February 1437, and he was crowned on 25th March 1437, at Hollyrood Abbey, Edinburgh. James II was only six years old when his father was murdered at Perth. When he was ten, his advisers had the young sixth Earl of Douglas and his brother murdered at 'The Black Dinner' in 1440, at Edinburgh Castle. In 1452, James himself stabbed the eighth Earl to death during a violent quarrel in Stirling Castle, and later defeated the Douglass at Arkinholm. Three years later, the ninth Earl and his relatives were forfeited for treason, and in 1458, his Parliament congratulated James on suppressing dangerous law-breakers.

James II married on 3rd July 1449, at Holyrood Abbey, Edinburgh. Mary she was the daughter of Arnold, Duke of Gueldres, by Katherine, Daughter of Adolph, Duke of Cleaves, and she was born in 1433. She was crowned Queen consort, on 3rd July 1449, at Holyrood Abbey, Edinburgh. Mary she was a devout and cultivated person, throughout most of James's reign. She died on 16th November, or 1st December 1463, and was buried in the Holy Trinity Church, Edinburgh.

James II was killed on 3rd August 1460, at the siege of Roxburgh, when a cannon he stood next to exploded, killing him instantly at the age of 29, and he was buried in Holyrood Abbey, Edinburgh. His son James succeeded him.

He was born on 10 July 1451, at Stirling Castle; and was Duke of Rothesay from birth. He succeeded his father as King of Scotland on 3rd August 1460, (at the age of nine), and he was crowned on 10th August 1460, at Kelso Abbey, Roxburghshire. His mother ruled as Regent until her death in 1463. In 1469, James began to rule for himself, shortly after his marriage to Princess Margaret of Denmark, and her father, King Christian I of Denmark and Norway, had to give her a dowry of 60,000 florins but he could only raise 10,000, so he pledge his lands and rights in Orkney as security for the remainder. Unable to assemble the remainder in time, he had to pledge his possessions in Shetland as well. Most of the lands and revenues in the islands already belonged to the earldom of Orkney. In 1471, James III persuaded the Earl to exchange his property there for lands in Fife. Christian I was never able to raise the money, so Orkney and Shetland remained Scottish possessions.

His preference for the company of scholars, and artists infuriated his nobles, his own brothers, Alexander, Duke of Albany and John, Earl of Mar regarded him with jealousy, they even hated him. In 1479, James brothers where arrested on suspicion of conspiring against the Crown. The Earl of Mar died mysteriously, whilst the Duke of Albany escaped to England. Although James tried to settle his differences with the Duke of Albany, his brother again tried to win the kingdom, but failed, and he was exiled to France.

James' coinage was the first in Scotland or England to bear a true likeness of the monarch, and the ever-present English threat, was temporarily solved by a truce with Edward IV in 1463.

James III married on 10th/13th July 1469, at Holyrood Abbey, Edinburgh. Margaret she was the daughter of Christian I, King of Denmark, Norway and Sweden, by Dorothea, daughter of John III, Margrave and Elector of Brandenburg, and she was born between 1456/1457. She died on 14th July 1486, at Stirling Castle, and she was buried in Cambuskenneth Abbey, Stirlingshire.

James III he was assassinated, on 11th June 1488, (after being defeated by the Scottish nobles) by being thrown from his horse has he fled from the field, at the Battle of Sauchieburn, he was carried into a nearby cottage at Milltown, near Bannockburn, where a mysterious figure forced his way in, and exclaimed, 'I will shrive thee!' and stabbed him to death. James he was buried in Cambuskenneth Abbey, Stirlingshire. His son James succeeded him.

He was born on 17th March 1473, and was Duke of Rothesay, Earl of Carrack, and Lord of Cunningham probably from birth. He succeeded his father as King of Scotland on 11th June 1488, and was crowned on 26th of June 1488, at Scone Abbey, Perthshire. For the first time in a century, Scotland had a king who was able to start ruling at once for himself and his kingdom, he had wonderful powers of mind, an astounding knowledge of most everything, and he was known to be a very generous person.

He spoke Latin (at that time the international language), French, German, Flemish, Italian, Spanish and some Gaelic, and took an active interest in literature, science and the law, even trying his hand at dentistry and minor surgery. It was not long after the printing press came to Scotland, when the Royal College of Surgeons in Edinburgh were founded. St Leonard's College, St Andrews, King's College. By 1493, he had overcome the last independent lord of the Isles, after extended royal administration to the north and west.

On 8th August 1503, 'The Marriage of the Thistle and the Rose' took place at Holyrood Abbey. This match had great significance, especially after the death of Elizabeth I of England, and the end of the Tudor dynasty. Relations with England To begin with were very difficult. In 1495, James supported Perkin Warbeck in his claim to the English throne; Even so, he was anxious to maintain peace with England. By 1502, he had finally concluded a peace treaty.

James became James I of Scotland & James VI of England. In 1513, England invaded France When Henry VIII joined the Holy Alliance against them, James then felt that he must assist Scotland's old ally under the 'Auld Alliance'. He led his army south, one of the largest ever to cross the border. Led by Lord Surrey the English forces inflicted a crushing defeat.

James IV married by proxy on 25th January 1502, at Richmond Palace, Surrey; and in person on 8th August 1503, at Holyrood Abbey Edinburgh.

Margaret she was the daughter of Henry VII, King of England, by Elizabeth of York, and she was born on 28th/30th November 1489, in the Palace of Westminster. She was crowned Queen Consort, on 8th August 1503, at Hollyrood Abbey, Edinburgh. After the death of James IV, she married Archibald Douglas, 6th Earl of Angus: she divorced him, and married Henry Stewart 1st Lord Methven. She died either on 8th/18th October, or 24th November 1541, at Methven Castle, Perthshire, of "cerebral Palsy", and she was buried in the Carthusian Abbey, Perth.

James IV died at the head of his men, with a large number of his nobles dieing with him, on 9th September 1513, in the disastrous Battle of Flodden, three miles southeast of Cold stream, Northumberland. His son James succeeded him.

James V

He was born either on 10th/11th or 15th April 1512, at Linlithgow Palace Fife, and was Duke of Rothesay from birth. He succeeded his father as King of Scotland on 9th September 1513, and he was crowned on 21st September 1513, at the Chapel Royal, Stirling Castle. He was appointed a Knight of the Garter, on 20th January 1535. When James IV was killed at Flodden; his son James V was only one year old.

The Scots, could, not accept his mother Margaret Tudor, as Regent, after her remarriage in 1514, so they replaced her with James IV's half-French cousin, the Duke of Albany. Moreover, after she divorced her second husband, Archibald Douglas 6th Earl of Angus, he left and took the young James with him, and held him captive for two years. James finally managed to escape in 1528, to rule by himself.

In 1536, he decided to marry Princess Madeleine of France, for he was eager to strengthen 'the Auld Alliance' against England, but she died in his arms on 7th July 1537, seven weeks after arriving in Edinburgh. In 1538, he married another French woman, Mary of Guise; she was a mother of two sons, she had two more sons by James but they both died in infancy within hours of each other in 1541.

Henry VIII, James V's uncle, broke with the Roman Catholic Church and dissolved the monasteries, urging James to do the same, James refused. In 1542, he was supposed to go to an arranged meeting with Henry at York, but James refused to go; Henry was Furious, and launched an invasion of Scotland. James then marched south with his army, and was defeated at the Battle of Solway Moss on the Scottish/English Border on 24th November 1542.

James himself had not been present at the battle of Solway Moss; he suffered a complete nervous collapse. Retreating to Falkland Palace in Fife, he took to his bed with a high fever. Then a message came telling him that his pregnant wife had given birth to a baby daughter. James himself hoping for a son believed that the Stewart dynasty was at an end, 6 days later, he was dead. James V first married on 1st January 1537, at the Cathedral of Notre Dame, Paris.

Madeleine she was the daughter of Francis I, King of France, by Claude daughter of Louis XII, King of France. She was born on 10th August 1520, at the Chateau of St Germain-en-Laye Paris. She died on 2nd/7th July 1537, at the Holyrood Palace, Edinburgh, where she was buried. There was no issue from this marriage.

James V married secondly by proxy in May 1538 and again in person on 12th June 1538, at St Andrews Cathedral Fife. Mary she was the daughter of Claude I, Duke of Guise-Lorraine, by Antoinette, daughter of Francis de Bourbon, Duke of Vendome, and she was born on 22nd November 1515, at Bar-le-Duc, France. She was crowned Queen Consort, on 22nd February 1540, at Holyrood Abbey, Edinburgh. She died on 10th/11th June 1560, at Edinburgh Castle, and she was buried in Rheims Cathedral France.

James V died on 14th December 1542, at Falkland Palace, Fife, and he was buried in Holyrood Abbey, Edinburgh. His daughter Mary succeeded him.

Queen Mary

She was born on 8th December 1542, at Linlithgow Palace West Lothian. She succeeded her father as Queen of Scotland, on the 14th December 1542, (she was only six days old) and she was crowned on 9th September 1543, at Stirling Castle. She became Queen Consort of France, on 6th July 1559, upon the accession of her first husband to the French throne. She was also next in line to the English throne, after Henry VIII children. Knowing this, the Scottish nobility decided that they must make peace with England, and they agreed that she should marry Henry VIII's son, the future Edward VI. However, the Catholics were opposed to this match, so they took the young Mary to Stirling Castle, preferring to return to Scotland's traditional alliance with France. This infuriated Henry and he ordered a savage series of raids into Scotland, known as 'The Rough Wooing'.

In 1548, Mary was betrothed to the French King Henry II's heir, the Dauphin of Francis, and he sent her to be brought up at the French Court, but in 1561, despite the warnings of her friends, Mary decided to go back to Scotland, and she returned to an unexpectedly warm welcome from her Protestant subjects. When the Dauphin succeeded to his father's throne in 1559, it made Mary, Queen of France as well as Scotland, but his reign was brief for he died of an ear infection in 1560.

At first Mary ruled successfully, but her marriage in 1565 to her second cousin Henry, Lord Darnley (great-grandson of Henry VII) it initiated a tragic series of events, Mary's enemies burst into her upper chamber, threatened her, (now heavily pregnant), and murdered her secretary, David Riccio, on 9th March 1566, inside the Palace of

Holyrood house. Darnley he was murdered at Kirk o'Field, just outside the walls of Edinburgh on 10th February 1567.

Her subsequent marriage three months later to the Earl of Bothwell (generally believed to be the principal murderer) brought her inevitable ruin. On 15th June 1567, she surrendered to her Protestant Lords that rose against her, at Carberry Hill near Edinburgh, and she was imprisoned in Lochleven Castle, Kinross-shire, she was then forced to abdicate in favour of her infant son James VI & I.

Bothwell fled to Scandinavia, where he was arrested and held prisoner until the day he died. In 1568, Mary escaped from Lochleven, and on 13th May 1568, she was defeated, at the Battle of Langside, near Glasgow.

Fleeing to England, in the hope that Queen Elizabeth I would support her cause, she didn't, instead she was kept her in captivity in England for nearly 19 years, wiliest she was there, Elizabeth's ministers demanded she should be executed.

Queen Mary married firstly on 24th April 1558, at the Cathedral of Notre Dame, Paris. Francis II he was the son of Henry II, King of France, by Catherine, daughter of Lorenzo de' Medici, Duke of Florence. He was born on 16th January 1544, at the Chateau of Fontainbleau-sur-Loire, Francs. He became King Consort of Scotland upon his marriage to Queen Mary. He succeeded his father, as King of France on 6th July 1559, and he was crowned; with Mary, on 18th September 1559, at Rheims Cathedral: he died on 5th December 1560, at Orleans, France, and he was buried in the Cathedral, of St Denis, Paris. There was no issue.

Queen Mary married secondly on 29th July 1565, in the Chapel of Holyrood Palace Edinburgh. Henry he was the son of Matthew Stewart, 4th Earl of Lennox, by Margaret, daughter of Archibald Douglas, 6th Earl of Angus, by Margaret Tudor, daughter of Henry VII of England: and widow of James IV. He was born on 7th December 1545, at Temple, Newsham, Yorkshire, and was Lord Darnel from birth. He was created Baron Ardmannoch and Earl of Ross on 15th May 1565, and was proclaimed King of Scotland, on 28th July 1565, but was normally referred to as King Consort. He was created Duke of Albany, on 20th July 1565. Henry he was murdered, with the help of Queen Mary herself, on 10th February 1567, at Provost's House, Kirk o'the Field, Edinburgh, and he was buried in Holyrood Abbey Edinburgh.

Queen Mary married thirdly on 15th May 1567, at Holyrood Palace, Edinburgh. James he was the son of Patrick Hepburn, 3rd Earl of Bothwell. He was born in 1535. He succeeded his father as fourth Earl of Bothwell in September 1556, and was created Duke of Orkney and Earl of Shetland on 12th of May 1567. His titles and estates were all declared forfeit, on 20th December 1567, because he left Mary, and married Jean, daughter of George Gordon, 4th Earl of Huntly, but they were divorced on the grounds of his adultery. James died on 14th April 1578, in prison at Dragsholm Castle, Denmark: and was buried in Faarevejle Church, Drags Holm Denmark.

Queen Mary was executed on 8th February 1587, (age 44) at Fotheringhay Castle, Northants, and was buried in Peterborough Cathedral. Her son James VI and I later exhumed her remains in 1612, and had her body placed in the vault of King Henry VII, Chapel in Westminster Abbey. Her son James succeeded her.

James VI & I

James VI and I he was the only son of Mary, Queen of Scots by her second husband, Lord Darnley. He was born on 19th June 1566, at Edinburgh Castle; he was Duke of Rothesay from birth. He succeeded his father as Duke of Albany, Earl of Ross and Baron Ardmannoch on 10th February 1567: he succeeded his mother as King of Scotland on 24th July 1567, and was crowned on 29th July 1567, at the Church of HolyRood, Stirling.

James VI & I succeeded Elizabeth I, (last of the Tudor sovereigns), as King of England on 24th March 1603, thus founding the Royal House of Stuart, and uniting the Crowns of England and Scotland under one Monarch, for the first time, henceforth, the Kingdom incorporating England and Scotland would be known as Great Britain.

James he was less than a year old when his mother died, and only thirteen months old when he was crowned, in Stirling, King of Scots, after her forced abdication. James he grew up to be a shrewd intellectual, after a demanding education by his tutor George Buchanan. He re-established friendly relations between him and his nobility, making him the most effective ruler Scotland ever had.

One of his greatest ambitions was to succeed Elizabeth I, to the throne of England, so he only made a formal protest when she signed his mother's death warrant in 1587. In 1589, he married Anne of Denmark; they had three sons and four daughters. On 24 March 1603 James achieved his lifelong ambition when Queen Elizabeth I died, he inherited the throne of England.

When he forced through the 1618 General Assembly, his Five Articles of Perth, were intended to bring the worship and government of the Church of Scotland into line with the Church of England. Realising that he had made an error of judgement, after he met with strong opposition, he did not enforce the Articles, and did not try to introduce them again. James he enjoyed the pomp and circumstance of the English court, and returned to Scotland only once, in 1617.

The house of Stewart

England and Scotland became a united, Kingdom in 1603, when James VI of Scotland became James 1 of England, that finally fulfilled Edward I dream, of the two countries being joined, under one monarch. James I he believed in the divine right of King's: that brought about dramatic changes in the nature of the monarchy. James believed that he was God's mouthpiece on earth and could do and say no wrong: this was also the view of his son Charles I, this angered the Parliament, when James tried to rule without them. He failed with this, and the country was plunged into the great civil war, thus ended in King Charles I execution and the declaration of a Republic under Oliver Cromwell, who became Lord Protector.

The monarchy survived of course, but Charles II had to live in exile, in Holland and France, while Cromwell was in government, but Crowell died in 1658, and his hold on the country died with him. Parliament then sent for Charles II, and his restoration came about in May 1660.

James VI & I married by proxy on 20th/24th August 1589, at Kronborg Castle, Copenhagen, Denmark, and in person on 23rd November 1589, at Oslo, Norway; and again in person on 21st January 1590, at Kronborg Castle. Anne she was the daughter of Frederick II, King of Denmark and Norway, by Sophia, daughter of Ulrich III, Duke of Mecklenburg-Gustrow, and she was born on 14th October, (not the 12th December 1574, as is sometimes stated) at Skanderborg Castle, Jutland, Denmark. She was Crowned Queen Consort on 17th May 1590, at Holyrood Abbey. Edinburgh: and was crowned Queen consort of England on 25th July 1603, in Westminster Abbey, She died on 4ᵗʰ March 1619, at Hampton Court Palace, and was buried in Westminster Abbey.

James VI & I he died on 27ᵗʰ March 1625, at Thoebalds Park, Herts, and was buried in Westminster Abbey. His son Charles succeeded him.

Charles I

He was born on 19ᵗʰ November 1600, at Dunfermline Palace, Fife; he was the second son of James VI, by Anne of Denmark. Charles he left Scotland in 1603, (at the age of three) and was brought up in the south after his father inherited the throne of England, and his only visit to Scotland, after his accession was in 1633, when he was crowned King of Scotland. He was created Duke of Albany, Marquees of Ormonde, Earl of Ross and Baron of Ardmannoch on 23ʳᵈ December 1600, and on 6ᵗʰ January 1605, he was created Duke of York, and appointed a Knight of the bath. He was appointed a Knight of the Garter on 24ᵗʰ April 1611. He succeeded his brother Henry as Duke of Cornwall and Rothesay, on 6ᵗʰ November 1612, and was created and invested as Prince of Wales and Earl of Chester on 4ᵗʰ November 1616, at Whitehall Palace, London. He succeeded his Father as King of Great Britain on 27ᵗʰ march 1625, and he was crowned, on 2ⁿᵈ February 1626, at Westminster Abbey; he was crowned again in Scotland, on 15ᵗʰ/18ᵗʰ June 1633, at Holyrood Abbey, Edinburgh.

After his initial successes at Perth, Aberdeen and Inverlochy; Montrose's forces were crushed at Philiphaugh in 1645. After his defeat at Naseby, Charles surrendered to the Scots in 1646 and entered into negotiation. The Scots then handed him over to the English and after further abortive negotiations with the English Parliament, Charles returned to talks with the Scots in December 1647. The Scots' agreement to provide an army to restore him, led to the second Civil War in the spring of 1648, which ended in Cromwell's victory at Preston. After the Civil War between the Cavaliers and Roundheads, Charles I, was tried, and condemned to death, by Oliver Cromwell, who had organised an illegally formed Parliament, and who convicted him of treason against the state.

Charles I married by proxy on 1ˢᵗ/11ᵗʰ May 1625, at the Cathedral of Notre Dame, Paris, and in person on 13ᵗʰ June 1625, at St Augustine's

Church, Canterbury, Kent. Henrietta Maria she was the daughter of Henry IV, of Bourbon, King of France, by Mary, daughter of Francis I de' Medici, Grand Duke of Tuscany. She was born on 26th November 1609, at the Palace of the Louvre Paris. She was never crowned Queen consort; being a Roman Catholic, she could not allow herself to become actively involved in the Anglican coronation ritual: she died on 21st/31st August 1669, at the Chateau of St Colombes near Paris, and was buried in the Cathedral, of St Denis, Paris.

Charles I was executed on 30th January 1649, outside Whitehall Palace, London, and he was buried in St George's Chapel Windsor. After his death, Britain was declared a republic, (for the first and only time in history) with Oliver Cromwell as Lord Protector. Charles, he was succeeded in name only by his son Charles, then in exile in France.

Charles II

The eldest surviving son of Charles I, he was only eight years old when Civil War broke out. He was born on 29th May 1630, at St James's Palace, London, and was Duke of Cornwall and Rothesay from birth. He was made a Knight of the Garter, on 21st May 1638, and was crowned probably the same day. He was designated Prince of Wales, and Earl of Chester, (but never created), in May 1649. He succeeded his father as King of Great Britain: (but in name only), on 30th January 1649. After the execution of Charles I, on 30th January 1649, the same day as he succeeded his father, Charles II was then in exile in France. Cromwell then took up the office of governing Britain under the title Lord Protector.

The Scots then rallied to Charles cause, but Cromwell marched north, defeated the Scots at the Battle of Dunbar on 3rd September 1650. On 1st January 1651, the Scots crowned Charles II at Scone Abbey Perthshire, (this turned out to be the last such Coronation at Scone). In July, the English army marched into Fife and then captured Perth, while the Scottish forces headed south into England, where they were defeated at the Battle of Worcester on 3rd September 1651. Charles II escaped, to France, the English then moved on to take Stirling and Dundee.

By 1st October, Scottish resistance was effectively at an end, and the English government announced that England and Scotland were henceforth to be one commonwealth. This union took effect from 1652, although the acts of union did not become law until 1657. In 1660, he was invited back to London, and he was restored to the throne of Great Britain, after nine years in exile. Cromwell died "of malaria" on 29th May I660, and Charles II was crowned on 23rd April 1661, at Westminster Abbey.

Charles II married on 21st/22nd May 1662, at the Church of St Thomas a Becket, Portsmouth. Katherine Henrietta she was the daughter of John IV, Duke of Braganza, and king of Portugal, by Louisa Maria, daughter of John Manuel Domingo Perez de Guzman, 8th Duke of Medina-Sidonia, and she was born on 15th/25th November 1638, at Vila Vicosa, Lisbon, Portugal. She was never crowned as Queen Consort because she was a Roman Catholic and could not bring herself to take part in an Anglican coronation ritual. She died on 30th November, or 1st December 1705, either at Belem Palace: or, Bemposta Palace, Lisbon, Portugal, and was buried in the monastery of Belem, Lisbon.

Charles II died on 6th February 1685, at Whitehall Palace, London, of the effects of a stroke, and he was buried in Westminster Abbey. His brother James succeeded him.

James II

He was born on 14th/24th October 1633, at St James's Palace, London, and he was designated Duke of York from birth. He was appointed a Knight of the Garter, on 20th April 1642, and created Duke of York on 27th January 1644, and Earl of Ulster on 10th May 1659. Louis XIV of France created him Duke of Normandy on 31st December 1660. He succeeded his brother Charles II as King of Great Britain on 6th February 1685, having changed to Roman Catholicism earlier. He was privately crowned by Catholic rites, on 22nd April 1685, at Whitehall Palace, London, and was crowned by the traditional Anglican ritual on 23rd April 1685, at Westminster Abbey.

James II was deemed by Parliament, to have abdicated on 11th December 1688, by leaving the country to exile in France, and was formally deposed by Parliament on 23rd December 1688.

James II first married in secret on 24th November, or 24th December 1659, at Breda, Holland (although doubts exist as to whether this ceremony ever took place at all), and publicly on 3rd September 1660, at Worcester House the Strand, London.

Anne she was the daughter of Edward Hyde, 1st Earl of Clarendon, by Frances, daughter of Sir Thomas Aylesbury, and she was born on 12th/22nd March 1637, at Cranbourne Lodge, Windsor. She died on 31st March 1671, at St James's Palace, London, of cancer, and she was buried in Westminster Abbey.

James II married secondly by proxy on 20th/30th September 1673, at the Ducal Palace, Modena, Italy, and in person on 21st November 1673, at Dover, Kent.

Mary Beatrice Eleanor Anne Margaret Isabelle, Baptized Maria, but called Mary from the day she was married. Mary she was the daughter of Alfonso d' Este III, Duke of Modena, by Laura, daughter of Girolamo Martinozzi, and she was born on 25th September, or 5th October 1658, at the Ducal Palace, Modena, Italy. She was crowned Queen Consort by Catholic rites on 22nd April 1685, at Whitehall Palace, London, and by Anglican rites no 23rd April 1685, at Westminster Abbey: she died on 7th/8th May 1718, at the Chateau of St Germain-en-Laye, Paris, of cancer, and was buried in the Abbey of St Mary, Chaillot, France. Her body was later destroyed, during the French revolution.

James II died on 16th September 1701, at the Chateau of St Germain-en-Laye, near Paris. His body was temporarily buried in the Chapel of St Edmund in the Church of the English Benedictines in the Rue St Jacques, Paris, whilst awaiting transportation to England for burial in Westminster Abbey. The body however, went missing during the French Revolution, but there were reports that it was found and reinterred at St Germain-en-Laye by order of George IV. An Interregnum followed the deposition of James II, who was succeeded two months later, by his son-in-law William of Orange, and his daughter Mary as joint Sovereigns.

William III and Mary II

William III

Baptized William Henry, he was the son of Princess Mary, daughter of Charles I, and he married his cousin, another Princess Mary, the daughter of James VII and II, by his Protestant first wife Anne Hyde. He was born on 4th/14th November 1650, at Binnenhof Palace, The Hague, Holland, and was Stadtholder of Holland from birth, his father having predeceased him. However, he had already been deprived of this title during his childhood. He was appointed a Knight of the Garter, on 25th April 1653. He was designated Count of Nassau-Dillenburg, and reinstated as Stadtholder of Holland in 1672.

William and Mary were proclaimed on 11 April 1689, and accepted the crown of Great Britain as joint sovereigns (Mary being the rightful heir) on the 11 May 1689, following the Interregnum after the abdication and deposition of his father-in-law James II, on 4th April 1689. William III, and Mary II, was crowned on 11th of April 1689, at Westminster Abbey. The same year 1689, they won a victory at Killiecrankie in Perthshire, but their leader Viscount Dundee was killed and they were crushed at Dunkeld, Even so, armed resistance continued in the Highlands until 1692, and the Bass Rock held out for James until April 1694. After Mary II died, William reigned alone: the rightful heir being Anne Stuart, who gave up her place in the succession for him to rule for the rest of his life.

William III was very unpopular in Scotland, after approving the 1692

Massacre of Glencoe, when the elderly chief of the MacDonald's of Glencoe failed to take the oath of allegiance to William by the appointed date, he was murdered with a number of his clansmen on government orders. William's callous disregard of those Scots who tried to set up a Scottish trading colony at Darien, on the Isthmus of Panama, led to widespread anger against him. William III married on 4th November 1677, either at St James's Palace, or Whitehall Palace, London.

Mary II she was born on 30th April 1662, at St James's Palace, London. She was proclaimed Queen of Great Britain on 13th February 1689, following the Deposition of her father and the Interregnum. She reigned as joint sovereign with her husband, with whom she was crowned, on 11th April 1689. She died childless on 28th December 1694, at Kensington Palace, London of smallpox, and she was buried in Westminster Abbey.

William III he died after a fall from his horse on 8th March 1702, at Kensington Palace, London, and he was buried in Westminster Abbey. Anne succeeded him in 1702.

Queen Anne

She was the younger daughter of James VII and II, by his first wife Anne Hyde, and she was born on 6th February 1665, at St James's Palace, London: she succeeded her brother-in-law William III, as Queen of Great Britain on 8th March 1702, and was crowned on 23rd April 1702, at Westminster Abbey. Her father was Lord High Commissioner at Holyrood house; she came to Scotland at the age of 15. In 1707, she adopted the royal style Queen of Great Britain, France and Scotland, following the Act of Union.

On 1 May 1707, the Treaty of Union came into effect, after months of bitter debate. The Hanoverian succession was thereby recognised, the rebellions were firmly quashed by the ruling House of Hanover, and there would in future be freedom of trade, the coinage, weights and measures would be the same, and Scotland would be represented in Parliament by 45 MPs and 16 elected peers. Queen Ann married on 28th July 1683, at the Chapel Royal, St James's Palace London.

George he was the son of Frederick III of Oldenburg, King of Denmark, by Sophia Amelia, daughter of George, of Brunswick-Luneberg. He was born either on 2nd April, 29th February, or the 21st April 1653, at Copenhagen, Denmark. He was naturalized has a British subject, on 20th September 1683, and appointed a Knight of the Garter on 1st January 1684. He was created Duke of Cumberland, Earl of Kendal and Baron of Wokingham, on 6th April 1689. During Queen Anne's reign, he was styled Prince George, never King Consort, he died on 28th October 1708, at Kensington Palace, London, and was buried in Westminster Abbey.

Queen Ann died on 1st August 1714, at Kensington Palace, London, she was the last of the Stuart monarchs, Sophia of Hanover having died only a few weeks previously, and so her eldest son George, Elector of Hanover now became George I of Great Britain. Although she conceived 19 children, her 18 pregnancies all ended in miscarriage, stillbirth or the birth of babies who did not live beyond childhood. Only William, Duke of Gloucester survived his earliest years, but he suffered from hydrocephalus and died five days after his eleventh birthday. Ann she was buried in Westminster Abbey, but she had no natural son or daughter to succeeded her, so it was her third cousin, Prince George of Hanover, who succeeded her.

When Queen Ann died, her nearest living Protestant relative was her third cousin, Prince George of Hanover, who was the grandson of Elizabeth Stuart, the Winter Queen, of Bohemia, and the daughter of James I. Elizabeth's daughter Sophia had married the Elector of Hanover, when the Act of Settlement was passed in 1701. Investing the succession in the House of Hanover, Sophia was still alive and hopeful of becoming Queen of Great Britain herself, in the fullness of time, but this was not to be, she died only weeks before Queen Anne passed away.

The House of Hanover

The House of Stuart still had members living in France, the children of James II. Prince James later changed his name to Francis Edward. He was a staunch Roman Catholic, and was barred from the succession, yet he still believed that he was the rightful King of Great Britain, and his supporters, known as Jacobites led an uprising on his behalf in 1715. It failed, so it was left up to his son, Bonnie Prince Charles to uphold the Jacobites claim, he failed in a second uprising in 1745, but the defeat of his supporters at Culloden, put an end for good any hopes of regaining the throne.

In exile in Italy, they still thought of themselves as King's of Great Britain: James III, Charles III, and Henry IX, (brother of Charles), but they were no longer a threat to the House of Hanover, and the line came to an end in 1807. The Hanoverians reined over Great Britain for nearly 200 years, with the succession passing peacefully from father to son, or even grandson, but finally, to the one and only, Queen Victoria.

George I   1714 - 1727

Baptized George Louis, he was born on 28th May, or 7th June 1660, at Osnabruck, Hanover. He succeeded his father as Duke and Elector of Hanover, on 23rc January 1698. He was appointed a Knight of the Garter, on 18th June 1701, and was naturalized as a British subject in 1705. He succeeded his third cousin, Queen Anne, as King of Great Britain, on 1st August 1714, and adopted the styled King of Hanover on the same day. He was crowned on 20th October 1714, in Westminster Abbey.

George I spoke German, French, and a little English. To fulfil his duties in Hanover George had to visit regularly, but with family tensions, and political differences, George imprisoned his wife in 1694. This had led to intense dislike between George and his son, George by 1719. In 1720, during the King's absences in Hanover power was delegated to the Regency Council and not to the Prince of Wales.

After 1717, George rarely attended Cabinet meetings. This allowed the Cabinet to act collectively and formulate policies, which left the king powerless, to resist if a majority backed the policies. In 1720, when the South Sea Company crashed (leaving the government and royal investments, with heavy loses), Robert Walpole took over. He was the most able of George's ministers, and known as the first 'Prime Minister'. Walpole was the longest running administrator in British history (1721-1742).

George I married on 21ˢᵗ November 1682, at Celle Castle Chapel, Germany. Sophia Dorothea she was the daughter of George William, Duke of Brunswick-Luneberg-Celle, by Eleanor, Countess of Williamsburg, daughter of Alexander II d'Olbreuse, Marquess of Desmiers, and she was born either on 3ʳᵈ February, 5ᵗʰ September, or 15ᵗʰ September 1666, at Celle Castle, Germany. Sophia was divorced by Prince George on 28ᵗʰ December 1694, because of her adultery, with Count Philip Christopher von konigsmarck. She was forbidden to remarry, and was confined to the Castle of Ahlden for the rest of her life, being styled Duchess of Ahlden from February 1695. She was never Queen of England. She died on 2ⁿᵈ/13ᵗʰ November 1726, at the Castle of Ahlden, Hanover, Germany, and she was buried in Celle Church, Germany.

George I died of the effects of a stroke, on 28ᵗʰ May, or 11ᵗʰ June 1727, during a visit to Osnabruck, Hanover, and was buried in the chapel of the Leine Schloss, Hanover. His body was transferred to the Chapel vaults of Schloss Herrenhausen after the Second World War, his son George succeeded him.

George II   1727 – 1761

Baptised George Augustus, he was born on 30ᵗʰ October, or 9ᵗʰ November 1683, at Schloss Herrenhausen, Hanover. He was naturalized as a British subject, in 1705, and appointed a Knight of the Garter on 4th April 1706. He was created Duke and Marquess of Cambridge, Earl of Milford Haven, Viscount of Northallerton, and Baron of Tewkesbury on 9th November 1706. He became Duke of Cornwall and Rothesay, when his father succeeded to the throne of Great Britain on the 1st August 1714. He was created and invested Prince of Wales and Earl of Chester, on 27th September 1714, at the Palace of Westminster. He succeeded his father as King of Great Britain on 28th May, or 11th June 1727, and was crowned on 11th October 1727, in Westminster Abbey.

George II was 60 years old, (the last British sovereign to fight in battle), when he last fought alongside his soldiers in 1743, at the Battle of Dettingen in Germany, against the French. For much of his reign George's political options were limited by the strength of the Jacobite cause. In 1745, George's reign was threatened when Charles Edward Stuart, the Young Pretender, landed in Scotland. After some success, he was finely defeated at the Battle of Culloden in April 1746 and the Jacobites threat was over.

The foundations of the industrial revolution were laid during George's reign, and trade was boosted by successes, such as Clive's victories in India and at Arcot in 1751; and at Plassey in 1757. This placed Madras and Bengal under British control, and in 1759, when Wolfe captured the French and held Quebec; it transferred Canada's wealthy trade in fish and fur from French to British rule.

George II married on 22nd August, or 2nd September 1705, at Schloss Herrenhausen, Hanover. Wilhelmina Charlotte Caroline she was the daughter of John Frederick, Margrave of Brandenburg-Ansbach, by Elenanor Erdmuthe Louisa, daughter of John George, Duke of Saxe Eisenach. She was born on 1st/2nd or the 11th March 1683, at Ansbach, Germany, and she was crowned on the 11th October 1727, at Westminster Abbey. Wilhelmina died on 20th November 1737, at St James's Palace, London, and she was buried in Westminster Abbey. George II died on 25th October 1760, at Kensington Palace, London, and he was buried in Westminster Abbey. His grandson George succeeded him.

George III ᛁ761 - 1821

Baptised George William Fredrick, he was the eldest son of Frederick, Prince of Wales, by Princess Augusta of Saxe-Gotha. He was only the third Hanoverian monarch, and the first one to be born in England, and to use English as his first language. He was born, on 4th June 1738, at Norfolk House, St James's Square London. He was appointed a Knight of the Garter, on 22nd June 1749. He succeeded his father as Duke of Cornwall, and Rothesay, Duke of Edinburgh, Marquess of the Isle of Ely, Earl of Eltham, Viscount of Launceston", and Baron of Snowdon on 20th March 1751. He was created Prince of Wales, Earl of Chester on 20th April 1751. He succeeded his grandfather George II as King of Great Britain, on 25th October 1760. He was crowned on 21st/22nd September 1761, at Westminster Abbey. On the 1st January 1801, he gave up for good the title "King of France", held by English Kings since Edward III laid claim to the French crown in 1340.

George III is remembered for two things: going mad and losing the American colonies. This is far from being true; he opposed their bid for independence to the very end. What he neglected to do was develop the policies, such as the Stamp Act of 1765 and the Townshend duties of 1767 on tea, paper and other products, this would probably have had support of Parliament, but instead led to war in 1775/1776. On 4th July 1776, American Independence Day, meant the end of the war, with the surrender of British forces in 1782.

George III he was one of the most appealing of the Hanoverian monarchs, and he was a good family man, after having 16 children, the third one a miscarriage, which occurred in the summer of 1764, at Richmond, Lodge, Surrey. George was still very devoted to his wife, Charlotte, for whom he bought the Queen's House which, was later enlarged to become Buckingham Palace.

George III is though to have married in secret, on 17th April 1759, Hannah Lightfoot, "a quakeress", daughter of a Wapping shoemaker, who is said to have borne him three children. Documents relating to the marriage, with the Prince's signature on them, were taken away and examined in 1866, by the Attorney General and he found they were genuine; they were then placed in the Royal Archives at Windsor.

In 1910, permission was refused an author who asked to see them. If George did make such a marriage when he was Prince of Wales, before the passing of the Royal Marriages act in 1772, then his subsequent marriage to Queen Charlotte was bigamous. That would make every monarch of Britain since a usurper. The rightful heirs of George III would have been his children by Hannah Lightfoot, if they ever existed.

George III married bigamously or not, on 8th September 1761, at the Chapel Royal, St James's Palace, in London. Sophia Charlotte known as Charlotte, she was the daughter of Charles Louis Frederick, Duke of Mecklenburg-Strelitz, by Elizabeth Albertine of Saxe-Hildburghausen, and she was born on 19th May 1844, at Mirow, Mecklenburg-Strelitz, Germany. On 7th March 1760, she was invested as a Protestant canoness of Herford (or Hervorden) in West phalli, Germany. She was crowned Queen Consort on 21st/22nd September 1761. She died on 17th November 1818, at Kew Palace, Surrey, and she was buried in St George's, Chapel, in Windsor.

George III After serious bouts of illness in 1788/1789 and again in 1801, he became permanently deranged in 1810. He suffered from the disease porphyries, which led his contemporaries to believe he was mad. In 1810 when his youngest daughter Amelia died on 2nd November 1810, at the age of 27, it broke his heart, and he became unfit to reign. In 1811, his son George was created Prince, Regent, and kept the title until his father's death, when he succeeded him. George he died on, 29th January 1820, at Windsor Castle, and he was buried in St George's Chapel Windsor. His son George succeeded him.

George IV 1821 – 1831

Baptized George Augustus Frederick, he was born on 12th August 1762, at St James's, Palace, London, and he was duke of Cornwall and Rothesay, Earl of Carrick, Baron Renfrew and Lord of the Isles from birth. He was created Prince of Wales and Earl of Chester, on 17th/19th August 1762. He was created Prince Regent of a United Kingdom by Act of Parliament on 5th February 1811, (at the age of 48) because of his father's incapacity: he held the title until his accession. He succeeded his father as King of Great Britain on 29th January 1820, and he was crowned on 19th July 1821, at Westminster Abbey.

George he was a very extravagant, collector and builder, and he acquired many important works of art, which are now in the Royal

Collection. He transformed Windsor Castle and Buckingham Palace into what they are today, and after his father's long illness, George started his royal visits again. In 1821, he visited Hanover, it had not been visited by the Royals since the 1750s, and he visited Scotland, and Ireland, over the next two years.

George IV first married on 15th September 1785, privately and in contravention of the Act of settlement 1701, and the Royal Marriages Act 1720, at her house in Park Lane, Mayfair London.

Maria Anne she was the daughter of Walter Smythe of Brambridge, by Mary, daughter of John Errington of Red Rice, Andover, Hants, and she was born on 26th July 1756, at Brambridge, Hants. Her marriage to the Prince of Wales was not valid under British Law, but was recognized by Papal Brief in 1800. Maria spent most of her life living apart from him, but she did remarry, firstly to Edward Weld, of Lulworth Castle, Dourest in 1775, and secondly to Thomas FitzHerbert of Norbury Derby in 1778. She died, on 27th/29th March 1837, at Brighton, Sussex, and was buried in the R. C. Church, of St John the Baptist, Brighton, Sussex; there was no issue between George and Maria.

George IV married secondly on 8th April 1795, at the Chapel Royal, St James's Palace London. Caroline Amelia Elizabeth she was the daughter of Charles II (William Ferdinand), Duke of Brunswick-Wolfenbuttel, by Princess Augusta of Wales: granddaughter of George II. She was born on 17th May 1768, at Brunswick, Germany. The King tried unsuccessfully to divorce her for adultery, (then a treasonable crime on the part of his Consort), and she was refused admission to his coronation in 1821. She died on 7th August 1821, at Brandenburg House, Hammersmith, London, and was buried in Brunswick Germany.

George IV died (age of 67) on 26th June 1830, at Windsor Castle, where he spent his final years in seclusion, and he was buried in St George's Chapel, Windsor. His brother William succeeded him.

William IV 1831-1837

Baptised William Henry, he was born on 21st August 1765, at Buckingham Palace. He was made a Knight of the Thistle, on 5th April 1770, and a Knight of the garter on 19th April 1782. He was created Duke of Clarence and St Andrews, and Earl of Munster on 20th May

1789: he succeeded his brother George IV as King of Great Britain on, 26th June 1830, and was crowned on 8th September 1831, in Westminster Abbey. In 1789, at the age of 13, he became a midshipman and started a career in the Royal Navy. He was made duke of Clarence in 1789, and retired from the Navy in 1790. Between 1791, and 1811, he lived with his mistress, the actress Mrs Jordan. In 1818, when his older brother died he became heir apparent at the age of 62. William IV married on 13th July 1818, at Kew Palace, Surrey.

Adelaide Louisa Theresa Caroline she was the daughter of George I (Frederick Charles), Duke of Saxe-Meiningen, by Louisa Eleanor, daughter of Christian Albert Louis, Prince of Hohenlohe-Langenburg, and she was born on 13th August 1792, at Meiningen, Thuringia, Germany. She was crowned Queen Consort on 8th September 1831, at Westminster Abbey. She died on the 2nd December 1849, at Bentley Priory, Stanmore, Middlesex, and she was buried in St George's Chapel, Windsor. Adelaide had five children to William, but they all died in infancy. William also had 11 illegitimate children, by a Caroline von Linsingen.

William IV died a month after Victoria had come of age, (thus avoiding another regency), on 20th June 1837, at Windsor Castle, and he was buried in St George's Chapel, Windsor. His niece Victoria succeeded him.

Queen Victoria 1837 - 1901

Baptized Alexandrina Victoria, she was born on 24th May 1819, at Kensington Palace London. She was the only daughter of Edward, Duke of Kent, the forth son of George III. She succeeded William IV her uncle, as Queen of Great Britain, on 20th June 1837, and she was crowned on 28th June 1838, at Westminster Abbey. She was declared Empress of India on 1st May 1876, and she was proclaimed as such on 1st January 1877 in Delhi, India.

Queen Victoria had three uncles who were ahead of her in succession - Frederick Duke of York, George IV, and William IV, but they had no legitimate children that survived, so she became Queen at the age of 18. Victoria she had a gift for drawing and painting, being educated she kept a diary, a regular journal about her life. She became Queen at the age of 18 in 1837. When Victoria married Prince Albert, in 1840, they brought up nine children, and most of them were married of into other royal families all over Europe, making her a very influential lady.

Victoria she was deeply in love with her husband, and she sank into a depression after he died in 1861. For the rest of her reign she only ever wore black, and until the late 1860s she rarely ever appeared in public; although she never neglected her official duties, but she did continue to give audiences to her ministers and official. In 1866 and 1867, she was persuaded to open Parliament in person. Between 1840 and 1882, seven attempts were made on Victoria's life, and her courage towards these attacks greatly strengthened her popularity: in 1868, it was the flattering attention of Benjamin Disraeli, the Prime Minister that helped her gradually to resume her public duties.

From 1874, to 1880, Victoria and her family started to travel quite widely, thanks to the improvements of transportation. Victoria was the first reigning monarch to travel on a train; she made her first train journey in 1842. There were other technical changes at the, time, such as newspapers, and the invention of photography. In her later years, she almost became the symbol of the British Empire. Both the Golden (1887) and the Diamond (1897) Jubilees, held to celebrate the 50th and 60th anniversaries of her accession, were marked with extravagant displays and public ceremonies. Despite her advanced age, Victoria continued her duties to the end, including an official visit to Dublin in 1900.

Queen Victoria married on 10th February 1840, at the Chapel Royal, St James's Palace London. Albert Francis Charles Augustus Emmanuel he was the son of Ernest I. Duke of Saxe-Coburg and Gotha, by Louise of Saxe- Gotha-Altenburg, and he was born, on 26th August 1819, at the Marble Hall Schloss Rosenau, Coburg, Germany. He was appointed a Knight of the Garter on 16th December 1839, and he was created Prince Consort on 26th June 1857. He died on 14th December 1861, at Windsor Castle, of typhoid, and was buried in St George's Chapel Windsor, in the Albert Memorial Chapel: his remains were later removed to the Royal, Mausoleum Frogmore in Windsor.

Queen Victoria died (at the aged of 82) on 22nd January 1901, at Osborne House, Isle of Wight, and she was buried in the Royal Frogmore mausoleum, Windsor, which she had built for her final resting place, beside her beloved Prince Albert, after a reign, which lasted almost 64 years, the longest in British history. Above the Mausoleum door there's an inscription in Victoria's words, 'farewell best beloved, here at last I shall rest with thee, with thee in Christ I shall rise again'. Her son Albert, who styled himself Edward VII, succeeded her.

The House of Saxe-Coburg-Gotha Becomes the House of Windsor

The Hanoverian line ended with the death of Queen Victoria, her son, Edward VII, was the first sovereign of the Royal House, of Saxe-Coburg- Gotha. At the turn of the 20ᵗʰ century, the British royal family was enjoying its greatest height of prestige, with the British Empire, which vastly expanded during the reign of Queen Victoria, covering much of the world. The Monarchy now had Imperial status, and Victoria herself made the best of all its greatest ideals.

The 20ᵗʰ century has seen the most dynamic changes in the history of the British Empire. As well as going through two world wars, the British Empire did not long survive the second, so it became the British Commonwealth of Nations, many of which have become independent since. It is ironic that the monarchy that led the British Empire through two wars against Germany should be of German origins, and its people closely intermarried with high-ranking supporters, such as Kaiser, William II or even Adolph Hitler. Even Queen Victoria spoke English with a strong German accent; she even spoke German at home with Albert. Yet so anti German was the feeling of the people. In 1917, King George V decided to eliminate all German names and titles from his house and family.

This is when the house of Saxe-Coburg-Gotha became the house Windsor. Mountbatten and Windsor were to become linked by marriage, some thirty years later, when Queen Elizabeth II married Lieutenant Philip Mountbatten. Since Elizabeth II accession, the house and family, are still known as Windsor, her children are surnamed

Mountbatten-Windsor. As most of us know, the monarchy has had to adapt to changes, especially with the media intrusion, trying to reduce it to the level of a soap opera, this is probably one of the worst threats the Monarchy as had to face since 1936, when Edward VIII abdicated to marry a twice-divorced woman. Only with the dedication and devotion to duty of King George VI, and no doubt with help of the Queen mother, set things back on an even keel.

The Queen herself continues with that tradition, and, as been rewarded with all the love and respect of her people. With her commitment to family life and tradition, she embodies all the domestic virtues of so successful a monarch. Queen Elizabeth II is a very visible monarch, seen to be performing her duties with sincerity and dedication, in the full glare of the public media; that makes her "to me" the Queen of excellence, and may she live a long and prosperous life.

As long as the Queen dose not abdicate; the succession is assured long into the 21st century, and we can hope with confidence, that the traditions of a thousand years of British monarchy will continue, long into the future.

Edward VII 1901 -1910 ·

Baptized Albert Edward, he was born on 9th November 1841, at Buckingham Palace, and was Duke of Cornwall and Rothesay, Earl of Carrick, Lord of the Isles, and Baron Renfrew from birth. He was created Prince of Wales and Earl of Chester on 8th December 1841, and Earl of Dublin on 17th January 1850. He was appointed a Knight of the Garter, on 9th November 1858. In 1863, he renounced his courtesy title, Duke of Saxe-Coburg Gotha inherited from his father. He was appointed a Knight of the Thistle on 24th May 1867: he succeeded his mother as King of Great Britain and Emperor of India on 22nd January 1901, and was crowned on 9th August 1902, at Westminster Abbey.

Edward's parents brought him up very strictly, and under a rigorous educational regime, and he undertook quite a number of public duties, as well as working on Royal Commissions in the field of social issues. It wasn't until 1898; his mother stopped him from acting as her deputy, having been heir apparent for longer than anyone else in British history: and it wasn't until he was 59 before he became king in 1904.

Edward was Fluent in French and German, and he made a number of visits abroad, mainly to France. His main interests lay in foreign affairs, and military and naval matters. He was related to nearly every Continental sovereign, and was known as the 'Uncle of Europe. Edward VII married on 10th March 1863, at St George's Chapel, Windsor.

Alexandra Caroline Marie Charlotte Louise Julie she was the daughter of Christian IX, King of Denmark, by Louise Wilhelmina Frederica Caroline Augusta Julie, Daughter of William X, Landgrave of Hesse-Cassel, and she was born on 1st September 1844, at the Amalienborg or "Gule" (yellow) Palace, Copenhagen, Denmark. She was appointed a Lady of the Garter in 1901, and was crowned Queen of Great Britain on 9th August 1902, at Westminster Abbey, she died on the 20th November 1925, at Sandringham House, Norfolk, and was buried in St George's Chapel Windsor.

Edward VII. In the last year of his life, he was involved in the constitutional crisis that was brought about by the refusal of the Conservative majority in the Lords, to pass the 1909, Liberal budget, but he died on 6th May 1910, at Buckingham Palace, before the situation could be resolved by the Liberal victory in the election of 1910. Edward was buried in St George's Chapel, Windsor. His son George succeeded him.

George V 1910 - 1936

Baptized George Frederick Ernest Albert, his reign began were his father left of, amid the continuing constitutional crisis over the House of Lords. The Bill was finely passed by the Lords in 1911, without having to organise and set up a mass of peers. George he was born, on 3rd June 1865, at Marlborough House, London. He was appointed a Knight of the Garter, on 4th April 1884, and was created Duke of York, Earl of Inverness and Baron Killarney on 24th May 1892. He became Duke of Cornwall and Rothesay when his father succeeded to the throne, on 22nd January 1901, and he was created Prince of Wales and Earl of Chester, on 9th November 1901. He succeeded his father as King of Great Britain and Emperor of India on 6th May 1910, and was crowned on 22nd June 1911, at Westminster Abbey: he was crowned Emperor of India on 11th December 1911, at New Delhi, India.

George V he was the only King-Emperor ever to visit India. In 1917, George V was persuaded by Germany to adopt the family name of Windsor, (after the Castle Windsor) so he changed the name of his House from Saxe- Coburg-Gotha to Windsor, and it remains the same today. When the First World War broke out in 1914, George made at least 450 visits to troops, and at least 300 visits to hospitals, visiting wounded servicemen. In the late 19th century, Support for Ireland's home rule had grown, but this was resisted by the Conservative Party and by the Unionists in the north. The 1916 Easter Rising in Dublin, and the occurring civil war, resulted in the setting up of the Irish Free State, to be known later as the Irish Republic.

In 1922, with the six northern counties remaining part of the United Kingdom George played a Conscious part in this, and on other occasions, such as the General Strike of 1926. In 1924, George readily welcomed the first Labour government, and he persuaded the Labour leader to head a National Government with all parties present, thus wining the election of 1931. In 1932, George started the first yearly Christmas Broadcast to the Empire (known today as the Commonwealth). George V married on 6th July 1893, at the Chapel Royal, St James's Palace.

Victoria Mary Augusta Olga Pauline Claudia Agnes known as Mary (or May within her family), she was the daughter of Francis Paul Charles Louis Alexander, Duke of Teck, by Princess Mary Adelaide of Cambridge, a granddaughter of George III, and she was born on the 26th May 1867, at Kensington palace, London. Before she married her husband, she was actually betrothed to his elder brother, the Duke of Clarence, but he died on 14th January 1892. She was appointed a Lady of the Garter in 1910, and she was crowned on 22nd June 1911, at Westminster Abbey; she was also crowned Empress of India on 11th December 1911, at New Delhi, India. Mary she died on 24th March 1953, at Marlborough House, London, and she was buried in St George's Chapel, Windsor.

George V in 1935, he celebrated his Silver Jubilee, but he sadly died the following year, on 20th January 1936, at Sandringham House, Norfolk, and he was buried in St George's Chapel, Windsor. His son Edward succeeded him.

Edward VIII 1936 - 1936

Baptized Edward Albert Christian George Andrew Patrick David, he was born on 23rd June 1894, at White Lodge, Richmond Surrey. He inherited the title Duke of Cornwall and Rothesay, Earl of Carrick, Lord of the Isles, and Baron Renfrew upon his father's accession to the throne, on 6th May 1910. He was appointed a Knight of the Garter on 23rd June 1910, and created Prince of Wales and Earl of Chester on the same day; being invested as such on 13th July 1911, at Caernarvon Castle, Wales. He was appointed a Knight of the bath in January 1936, and he succeeded his father as King of Great Britain and Emperor of India, on 20th January 1936.

Edward he was never crowned, his reign only lasted 325 days. Edward he abdicated on 11th December 1936, because he preferred to marry a woman who had been married and divorced twice before; an American Lady called Mrs Simpson, and when she obtained a divorce in 1936, it was clear that Edward was determined to marry her. Eventually Edward realised he had to choose between the Crown and Mrs Simpson. With him being the head of the Church of England such a marriage could not be condoned.

Edward he was created Duke of Windsor on 8th March 1937, he had already been designated four months before on 12th December 1936. Edward, he spent the rest of his life in exile in France, except for the occasional visits to England and sometimes America. During the Second World War, the Duke of Windsor escaped from Paris, (where he was living at the time of the fall of France), to Lisbon in 1940.

Edward was then appointed Governor of the Bahamas, a position he held until 1945. In 1936, Edward created The King's Flight (now known as 32

The Royal Squadron) after he qualified as the first monarch to become a pilot, and in 1936, he was the first to provide air transport for the Royal family's official duties.

Edward VIII married on 3rd June 1937, at Chateau de Cande, Maine- et-Loire, France, after his abdication. Bessie Wallis known as Wallis, she was the daughter of Teackle Wallis Warfield by Alice M. Montague, and she was born on 19th June 1896, at Square Cottage, the Monterey Inn, Blue Ridge Summit, Pennsylvania, U. S. A. Bessie Wallis, she married three times. The other two marriages, was firstly.

Earl Winfield Spencer on 8th November 1916, and divorced on 10th December 1927, secondly Ernest Aldrich Simpson, on 21st July 1928, and divorced on 27th October 1936. She died, on 24th April 1986, at home in the Bois de Boulogne, Paris, and was buried at Frogmore, Windsor. She never had any children to either of her marriages. Edward VIII died on 28th May 1972, at his home in the Bois de Boulogne, Paris of cancer, and he was buried in Frogmore, Windsor. His brother Albert succeeded him in 1936, using his last name George.

George VI 1936 - 1951

Baptized Albert Frederick Arthur George, he was born on 14th December 1895, at York Cottage Sandringham, Norfolk. He was appointed a Knight of the Garter in 1916, and was created Duke of York, Earl of Inverness and Baron Killarney, on 4th June 1920. He succeeded his brother Edward VIII, as King of Great Britain and Emperor of India, on 11th December 1936, and he was crowned on 12th May 1937, at Westminster Abbey. He gave up the title Emperor of India on 22nd June 1947, when India was granted independence.

George he was not expecting to become King, because of his brothers situation, and him being a conscientious and dedicated man, had to work hard to adapt to the role into which he was suddenly thrown. In 1938, he paid a State Visit to France, and in 1939, to Canada and the United States (he was the first British monarch to set foot on American soil with his family). During the Second World War he spent most his time at Buckingham Palace, where he had close working relationship with the Prime Minister, Winston Churchill.

When most of Europe fell to Nazi Germany in 1940, he initiated the George Cross and George Medal, these were to be awarded for acts of bravery. The George Cross was awarded to the island of Malta, for the heroism of the people resisting the enemy siege. During the First World War he served in the Navy, and actually fought at the Battle of Jutland, and the King was always willing and able to visit his troops whenever possible. He visited North Africa in 1943 after the victory of El Alamein, and in June 1944, he visited his Army on the Normandy beaches 10 days after D-Day.

On the eighth of May 1945, (V. E. day), links between the King and his people had become immeasurably strengthened. In 1947, accompanied by the Queen and their daughters, Princess Elizabeth and Princess Margaret, he went on a tour to South Africa, the first time for a sovereign and his family. In 1947, India and Pakistan became independent; and George had to give up the title Emperor of India.

George VI married on 26th April 1923, at Westminster Abbey. Elizabeth Angela Marguerite she is the daughter of Sir Claude George Bowes- Lyon, 14th Earl of Strathmore and Kinghorne, by Nina Cecilia, daughter of the Rev Charles William Frederick Cavendish-Bentinck. She was born on 4th August 1900, at Belgrade Mansions, Grovesnor Gardens, London, or it could have been in a London ambulance on the way to a London maternity home, as far as we know, the Queen mother herself believes she was born in an ambulance. She was appointed a Lady of the Garter in 1936, and was crowned Queen Consort and Empress of India on 12th May 1937, in Westminster Abbey. On the death of King George, she assumed the title of H. M. Queen Elizabeth the Queen Mother. She died, peacefully in her sleep at the ripe old age of "101", on 30th March 2002, at Royal Lodge, Windsor.

Prince Charles her grand son was "devastated", The Queen Mother's niece Lady Margaret Rhodes, was with her when she died, said: "It was a very moving and very sad moment but luckily it was peaceful." The Prime Minister Tony Blair led tributes by saying the Queen Mother had been a symbol of Britain's "decency and courage". After the death of her husband, The Queen Mother continued her public duties in the UK and overseas, which included over 40 official visits abroad, and a visit to Canada in 1989, marked the 50th anniversary of her first visit there.

Her Majesty was Patron or President of some 350 organisations. She was Commandant-in-Chief of the Army and Air Force Women's Services, and for Women in the Royal Navy, and held other Service appointments. For many years she was President of the British Red Cross Society, and she was Commandant-in-Chief of the Nursing Division of the St John Ambulance Brigade. She was also Colonel-in-Chief or Honorary Colonel of many UK and overseas regiments, and Commandant-in-Chief of the Royal Air Force Central Flying School.

Marking her 100th birthday in 2000, she attended a number of official engagements. These began on 27th June with a lunch at the Guildhall hosted by the Corporation of London. On 11th July followed a service of thanksgiving at St. Paul's Cathedral, and then a birthday pageant on Horse Guards Parade on 19th July. On her 100th birthday, she received, like all other centenarians, a message of congratulations from The Queen.

George VI died in his sleep after failing to recover from a lung operation on 6th February 1952, at Sandringham House, Norfolk, at the aged 56, he had cancer, and he was buried in the King George VI, Memorial Chapel, St George's Chapel, Windsor. His daughter Elizabeth succeeded him.

Queen Elizabeth II

Baptized Elizabeth Alexandra Mary Windsor, she was the first child of The Duke and Duchess of York, and she was born on 21st April 1926, at 17, Bruton Street, London. She succeeded her father as Queen of Great Britain, on 6th February 1952, and she was crowned on 2nd June 1953, at Westminster Abbey. In November 1947, she was created a Lady of the Garter. When she was born, it was unlikely that she would become Queen; it was because of certain events in the 1930s, which led to her father's Accession, and which resulted in her becoming next in line to the throne. The sudden accession of the Queen, in 1952, wasn't entirely unexpected; it was owing to King George VI, and his ill health, and sudden death of cancer.

For over 50 years now she has been our Queen, and like our selves she has seen a great number of social changes. As Head of State, she has carried out her responsibilities and political duties like the responsible Sovereign she is, and she as had an unprecedented programme of visits around the world, especially in the United Kingdom. In June 1947, on her return from a tour of South Africa, she received the freedom of the City of London, and in July 1947, she received the freedom of the city of Edinburgh.

On her succession to the throne, Her royal highness became head of the Navy, Army and Air Force of great Britain, and when she succeeded her father Elizabeth became Colonel-in-Chief of all the Guards Regiments; the Corps of Royal Engineers; Captain-General of the Royal Regiment of Artillery, and the Honourable Artillery Company.

The Queen's Golden Jubilee in 2002 was a very special milestone, achieved previously, by only five other British monarchs (King Henry III, King Edward III, King James VI and I, King George III, and Queen Victoria). To celebrate her Golden Jubilee, Her Majesty arranged two free public concerts for over 24,000 people in the gardens of Buckingham Palace, as well as an appearance before a crowd of one million people, on the balcony of Buckingham Palace. During the course of the year, The Queen and The Duke visited Australia, New Zealand, Jamaica and Canada. With the hope (and I'm sure) of the nation, she will live a long and prosperous life, much the same as her own mother.

Elizabeth II married on 20th November 1947, at Westminster Abbey. Philip he his the son of Prince Andrew of Greece and Denmark, by Victoria Alice Elizabeth Julia Marie, daughter of Louis, Prince of Battenberg, Marquees of Milford-Haven, and he was born on 10th June 1921, at Villa Mon Repose, Isle of Corfu Greece; the only son of Prince Andrew of Greece. (Prince Andrew being the grandson of King Christian IX of Denmark, and his mother Princess Alice of Battenberg, the eldest child of Prince Louis of Battenberg, and sister of Earl Mountbatten of Burma).

On the 28th February 1947, he gave up his Greek nationality and became a British subject, at the same time taking the surname Mountbatten. He was appointed a Knight of the Garter in 1947, and he was created Duke of Edinburgh, Earl of Marioneth and Baron Greenwich on 19th November 1947. He was appointed a Knight of the Thistle in 1952, on 27th February 1957, he was granted the title H. R. H. Prince Philip, with precedence over all other male members of the Royal Family.

Both the Queen and Prince Philip have Queen Victoria as a great-great grandmother, through Prince Louis marring one of Queen Victoria's granddaughters, his paternal grandfather, King George I of Greece, was Queen Alexandra's brother, relating them also through his father's side.

In 1928, Philip left his school in France, and came to England to attend Cheam Preparatory School, he left at 12 year old and went to Germany for one year, to attend School at Salem, and from there he went to Gordonstoun School in Morayshire, the same School his three sons attended. After becoming head of the School, he Captained the

Cricket and Hockey teem there, and being a keen sailor he took part in sailing expeditions to Norway, and around the coast of Scotland.

In 1949, he attending the Naval Staff College at Greenwich, after a short spell instructing in the Petty Officers' School, and was appointed First Lieutenant of H. M. S. Chequers; Leader of the First Destroyer Flotilla in the Mediterranean Fleet. In 1950, he was promoted to Lieutenant, Commander, and appointed commander of the Frigate H. M. S. MAGPIE, but on the death of his father in law, King George VI, his naval career ended. Although he gave up his naval career, in July 1951, he remains closely connected and actively interested in every branch of the Service.

In 1952, he was appointed Admiral of the Sea Cadet Corps, Colonel in Chief of the Army Cadet Force and Air Commodore in Chief of the Air Training Corps, and twelve month later he was promoted to Admiral of the Fleet, and appointed Field Marshal, and Marshal of the Royal Air Force, he is also Colonel, of a number of British and overseas regiments, and Captain- General of the Royal Marines.

he Duke of Edinburgh, has become Patron or President of some 800 organisations, since The Queen's accession, and has played a prominent part in many aspects of national life. His special interests are in scientific and technological research and development, the encouragement of sport, the welfare of young people, and conservation and the environment.

In 1952, he was made President of the British Association for the Advancement of Science, and with the aim of understanding British industrial life, he has visited research stations, laboratories, industrial plants, engineering works, coalmines and factories, making him familiar with every aspect of the UK's industrial life.

Prince Philip has served as Chancellor of four different Universities, Edinburgh in 1952, Wales 1948 to 1976, Cambridge 1976, and Salford 1967 to 1991; he is also Patron of London Guildhall University, and Life Governor of King's College, London.

Philip a keen sports man played polo regularly until 1971, a sport he took up while serving in Malta, and he has served twice as President of the Marylebone Cricket Club. He is also Admiral of the Royal Yacht Squadron, and from 1964 to 1986, he was President of the International Equestrian Federation. He is also Air Navigators of the British Empire, and Grand Master of the Guild of Air Pilots.

The formation of the World Wildlife Fund in 1961, Prince Philip was the first President until 1982, and from 1981 to 1996, he was International President of the World Wide Fund for Nature, he is to this day resident Emeritus of the World Wildlife Fund. Prince Philip as accompanied The Queen on all her tours and visits to all parts of the United Kingdom, and he accompanies her on all her Commonwealth tours and State Visits overseas. He also likes to travel abroad on his own account. He undertook around 578 engagements at home and abroad in 2002.

Issues of marriage:

Prince Charles

Baptized Charles Philip Arthur George, of Edinburgh, heir apparent to the throne, he was born on 14th November 1948, at Buckingham Palace. He inherited the title Duke of Cornwall under a charter of King Edward III dating back to 1337, which gave that title to the Sovereign's eldest son. In the Scottish Peerage, he also became, Duke of Rothesay, Earl of Carrick, Lord of the Isles, Baron Renfrew, and Prince, and Great Steward of Scotland, upon the Queens accession to the throne on 6th February 1952. He was created Earl of Chester and Prince of Wales, on 26th July 1958, and was invested as, on 1st July 1969, at Caernarvon Castle, Wales. He was appointed a Knight of the Garter in 1968, a knight of the Bath in 1976, and he was appointed a Knight of the Thistle in 1977. The Prince of Wales was appointed to the Order of Merit in June 2002.

Prince Charles he was educated in Scotland at both Cheam and Gordonstoun, and in 1966, Geelong Church of England Grammar School, in Melbourne, Australia, as an exchange student. He was the first member of the British Royal family to attend an overseas Commonwealth school. The Prince studied archaeology and anthropology, between 1967/1970, and in his last two years at the University of Cambridge, he studied history, and gained his University Colours ('half-Blue') for polo. In 1969, Charles spent one summer term in Aberystwyth at the University of Wales, and in 1970, he graduated from Cambridge with a B. A. Honours degree. The same year he took his seat in the House of Lords.

From 1971 to 1976, he served in the Royal Navy; his first Service appointment was as Colonel in Chief of the Royal Regiment of Wales, and in 1975, he became Colonel of the Welsh Guards, succeeding his father The Duke of Edinburgh. In 1971, he obtained his RAF wings, after spending six months at the Royal Air Force College at Cranwell, learning to fly jet aircrafts. In 1971, he joined the Royal Navy, doing his service on a guided-missile destroyer and two frigates. In 1974, he qualified as a helicopter pilot, and joined 845 Naval Air Squadron on Commando flying duties, which operated from the aircraft carrier H. M. S. HERMES. At the beginning of 1976 he took command of the coastal mine hunter H. M. S. BRONINGTON, by the end of 1976 he had left the Royal Navy, holding the rank of Vice-Admiral; Air Marshal in the Royal Air Force, and Lieutenant General in the Army.

Each year Prince Charles undertakes a large number of public engagements, both in England and oversees, and he takes a keen and active interest in all areas of public life. He is either associated as a patron or president of around 200 organisations, he has also a wide range of interests and activities, such as the unemployed, the disabled, young people, inner cities, education, the elderly, disabled, national heritage, environment, architecture, medicine, the arts, and sport.

He has a wide range of opinion, on national and international issues, and frequently has private meetings and discussions with Government Ministers with the business community, political figures, and academics, experts. Through the work of The Prince's Trust, which the Prince is President of, he has helped over 33,000 disadvantaged young people set up in business, and each year they collectively have a turnover of £60 million, employing over 2,000 staff. Prince Charles married on 29th July 1981, at St Paul's Cathedral, London.

Diana France she born on 1st July 1961, at Park House Sandringham Norfolk, she was the daughter of Edward John, 8th Earl Spencer, by the Honourable, Frances Ruth Burke, daughter of Edmund Maurice Roche, 4th Baron Fermoy. She was divorced, on 28th August 1996. She died, on 31st August 1997, in a road accident in France. She was the first Englishwoman, in more than 300 years, to marry an heir to the British throne.

Diana's educated began in Norfolk, at Riddlesworth Hall, preparatory school, she moved on to the West Heath School in Kent. Her finishing school was in Switzerland at Chateaux d'Oex at Montreux. Diana worked as a kindergarten teacher from 1979 to 1981, in Pimlico, London, a very exclusive Young England school. Her marriage to Prince Charles in 1981 was one of the most joyous occasions for the people of England, but by the late 1980s, the royal couple's marriage had become very strenuous, for both Princes Diana and Prince Charles.

In December 1992, a separation was announced, and in 1993, she briefly withdrew from public life. In early 1996, divorce proceedings began, and in August 1996, Diana and Charles were legally divorced. After the divorce, she would no longer, be permitted to use the title Her, Royal Highness, but on agreement, she would be known as Lady Diana, Princess of Wales. They had joint custody of their children.

Diana she actively supported many different charities, the homeless and deprived, breast cancer research, drug abuse, and aids. Being vice president of the British Red Cross, she served as a member of the International Red Cross advisory board, and in 1997, she visited Angola, Bosnia, and Herzegovina, to support the Red Cross campaign for the banishment of landmines.

When Diana died in 1997, a two-year investigation into the causes, (by the French judges) ruled that it had been caused solely by the over drinking of the driver, Henri Paul, and that decision cleared nine photographers of wrongdoing. Shortly after Diana's funeral, a memorial fund was established, that continued to fund the charities with which Diana was most involved.

Issues of marriage:

William Arthur Philip Louise

He was born on 21st June 1982, at St Mary's Hospital, Paddington, London, and is known as Prince William of Wales, second in line of succession to the throne.

Henry Charles Albert David

Known as Harry he was born on 15th September 1984, at St Mary's Hospital, Paddington, and he was christened by the Archbishop of Canterbury at Buckingham Palace, and is known as Prince Henry of Wales, third in line of succession to the throne.

Anne Elizabeth Alice Louise

Known as The Princess Royal, previously known as Princess Anne. the second child and only daughter of The Queen and The Duke of Edinburgh, she was born on 15th August 1950, at Clarence House, London, and was designated Princess Royal on 1st June 1987. The title Princess Royal was received from The Queen by Anne in June 1987, and is only the seventh holder of that title. In 1994, she was appointed a Lady of the Most Noble Order of the Garter, and to mark her 50th birthday, and in recognition of her work for charities, she was appointed to the Order of the Thistle.

The beginning of Ann's education started in 1952, in a small private class held at Buckingham Palace just after the sudden accession of the Queen. Buckingham Palace is where The Queen had moved with all her family shortly before. In 1962, she made a private educational visit to France, and in 1963, she went to Benenden School, a boarding school in Kent.

When she was eighteen, The Princess began to undertake, public engagements on her own. In 1969, she opened an educational and training centre in Shropshire, and in May the same year she accompanied her mother and father to Austria, on her first ever State Visit.

The princess as also devoted a large part of her working life to a wide range of charitable appointments. She has been the President of the Save the Children Fund since 1970, the first major charity with which she became closely associated; she was also closely involved with the creation of other charities, such as The Princess Royals Trust for Carers, Transaid and Riders for Health.

The Princess's great passion for riding, soon proved her an expert horsewoman. She regularly took part in the Horse of the Year Show at Wembley, and the Badminton Horse Trial, she won the individual

European Three-Day Event at Burghley In September 1971, and the same year she was voted the BBC's Sports Personality of the year. She was also nominated Sportswoman of the Year by the Sports Writers' Association, World Sport, and the Daily Express newspaper. She was also nominated by the journal of the British Olympic Association.

The Princess was also a member of the British team in the European Three-Day Event Championships at Kiev in the Soviet Union in 1973, and in 1975, she won silver medals as an individual competitor and as a team member in the same contest in Germany, and as a member of the British Three-Day Event team, she competed in the 1976 Montreal Olympic Games. This led to her becoming President of the British Olympic Association in 1983. The Princess also became one of the two UK members of the International Olympic Committee.

Since 1983, she has been an enthusiastic supporter of the British Olympic teams at successive games, including the highly successful games in Sydney in 2000. With the The Princess's interest in horses she as become closely involvement with many equine and veterinary charitable organisations, the most well-known is probably her presidency of Riding for the Disabled. The Princess has also written a book about her career, and love of horses, which is called 'Riding through My Life'. Anne first married on 14th November 1973, at Westminster Abbey, after nearly six months of engagement.

Captain Mark Anthony Peter Philips of The Queen's Dragoon Guards is the son of Major Peter William Garside M C, by Anne Patricia nee Tiarks, and he was born on 22nd September 1948. He and Ann were divorced on 28th April 1992.

In March 1974, after a charity film show The Princess, and Captain Phillips were being driven back to Buckingham Palace, along the mall, where there was an unsuccessful attempt made to abduct The Princess. She was unhurt, but during the incident her personal bodyguard was shot and wounded. He was later awarded the George Cross for his bravery.

Issues of marriage:

Peter Mark Andrew Phillips

He was born on 15th November 1977 at St Mary's Hospital, Paddington. He was christened by the Archbishop of Canterbury on 22nd December 1977; in the Music Room of Buckingham Palace.

Zahra Anne Elizabeth

She was born on 15th May 1981, at St Mary's Hospital, Paddington. She was christened by the Dean of Windsor on 27th July 1981; in the Chapel at Windsor Castle. Anne married secondly on 12th December 1992, at a private ceremony at Crathie Church, Scotland.

Commander Timothy Laurence he is the son of Guy Laurence by Barbara Symons, and he was born on 1st May 1955. Since his divorce he become, Commodore Laurence of the Royal Navy, (now Rear Admiral Laurence), there was no issue of his marriage to The Princess Royal.

Andrew Albert Christian Edward

He is the second son, and third child of Queen Elizabeth II, and The Duke of Edinburgh. He was born, on 19th February 1960, at Buckingham Palace, London. He was the first child in 103 years, to be born to a reigning monarch, and until he married, he was known as Prince Andrew; after is marriage, he was created Duke of York, Earl of Inverness, and Baron Killalee, on 23rd July 1986.

Prince Andrew married on 23rd July 1986, at Westminster Abbey. Sarah Margaret she is the daughter of Major Ronald Ivor Ferguson by Susan Mary, daughter of Fitzherbert Wright of Corbisdale Farm, Ardgay, Co. Ross, and she was born on 15th October 1959, at 27 Welbeck Street, London W.1.

Issue of marriage:

Beatrice Elizabeth Mary

She was born on 8th August 1988, at the Portland Hospital Great Portland Street, London, W.1.

Eugenie Victoria Helena

She was born on 23rd March 1990, at the Portland Hospital Great Portland Street, London, W.1.

Edward Anthony Richard Louise

He born on 10th March 1964, at Buckingham Palace and is known as H. R. H. Prince Edward, the third son and youngest child of The Queen and The Duke of Edinburgh, and is styled H. R. H. Prince Edward. Upon his marriage to Sophie, he was created Earl of Wessex and Viscount Severn. He will eventually succeed to the title of The Duke of Edinburgh.

Edward married on 19th June 1999, at St George's Chapel, Windsor Miss Sophie Rhys-Jones she is the only daughter of Mr and Mrs Christopher Rhys-Jones, and is known as H. R. H. the Countess of Wessex. She was born in Oxford, on 20th January 1965.

Issue of marriage:

Lady Louise Windsor

She was born on 8th November 2003.

That concludes the Royal family tree; hope that you have enjoyed this factual account of the Royals. If you would like to contact the author of this booklet, please email. geoffkeen31@gmail.com

Alphabetical Index

References

Weir.A. (1996) *Britain's Royal Families*. Revised edition. Great Britain, Kent: Mackays of Chatham PLC.

Lightning Source UK Ltd.
Milton Keynes UK
UKHW010616170420
361834UK00002B/4

9 781504 989794